# NOAH'S ARK
# NEW ENGLAND YANKEES

*AND*

# THE ENDLESS QUEST

*BY*

ROBERT KEITH LEAVITT

———————⊶◦◦◦⊷———————

*A SHORT HISTORY OF THE ORIGINAL WEBSTER DIC-*
*TIONARIES, WITH PARTICULAR REFERENCE*

*TO THEIR*

# FIRST HUNDRED YEARS

*AS*

*PUBLICATIONS OF*

# G. & C. MERRIAM COMPANY

SPRINGFIELD, MASSACHUSETTS

⧼⧽⧼⧽⧼⧽

1947

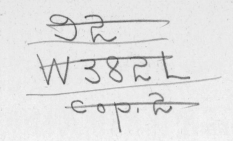
Copyright, *1947*, by *G. & C. Merriam Co.*

# FOREWORD

*SEPTEMBER 24, 1947, marks the hundredth anniversary of the first Webster dictionary to appear under the imprint of G. & C. Merriam Company. That volume was more than a mere reprint of Noah Webster's monumental tome; more, even, than an expansion of the immortal lexicographer's work by his literary heirs, adding to, revising, and keeping up to date the greatest dictionary of our language. It was the beginning of a cultural trusteeship, entered upon with deep purpose and maintained with high sincerity, unremitting zeal, and ever-increasing labor through all the years between.*

*It is fitting that at the end of our first century we should present an account of that trust. We have chosen to have the account prepared by a writer outside of our organization, free to form unbiased judgments, and to record the history of our custodianship, not as we might phrase it, but as the records show it to be. Mr. Leavitt has had access to all the files of this Company and of its predecessors, and to our collections of historical material which go back to the very sources of Noah Webster's work. We feel that he has written a readable and significant account not merely of this organization, but of the great cultural institution it has kept alive, fostered and increased, in trust for the knowledge of all mankind.*

G. & C. Merriam Company

# CONTENTS

# PART ONE

# Noah's Ark

N. Webster

Noah Webster, age sixty-five. Engraved from a portrait painted by
Samuel F. B. Morse in 1823.

# THIS WEBSTER

IN that soft and fragrant May of 1787, the city of Philadelphia was pleasantly thronged with distinguished visitors. The inns were filled, and the lodginghouses, and half the first families had thrown open their guest rooms, vying for the honor of entertaining the great men. For the Convention had met here — the Constitutional Convention — come "to form a more perfect Union" of a handful of jealous sovereign states that had just won a surprising war.

In the evenings, when the day's sessions were over and the people went out to take the air under the new-leafed trees, you could, often as not, rub elbows with some general of the Revolution, or a signer of the Declaration, or a member of the Continental Congress.

Dr. Franklin was there, of course, full of years and honors, and there were others by the score: Hamilton, Madison, the Morrises, the Pinckneys . . . delegates, advisers, observers, or just men who, having made history, came to see it made good. You might even catch a glimpse of the great Washington himself, first soldier, first citizen, unanimous choice for presidency of the Convention and unquestionably the only choice for chief of state of the new republic-to-be.

On the evening of May 26, 1787, General Washington went out and paid a call at the lodgings of another visitor. The object of this remarkable attention was no Revolutionary hero; he had served only briefly and abortively as a boy in a state guard contingent that started for Saratoga too late and then marched home again. He was no delegate to the Convention, nor even a special visitor for the occasion, but only a New Englander who happened to be teaching in Philadelphia. A youth not yet twenty-nine, he was hardly more than half Washington's age, and his worldly estate was so far below that of the great Virginia landowner that he could not even be certain of enough money to get married. And he had no social charm; indeed, from his youth people had considered him prosy and contentious; and his best friend, admirer, and patron in Philadelphia had to confess of him that his all-too-evident egotism alienated lecture audiences.

Yet General Washington had the soundest of reasons for calling to pay his respects to Noah Webster.

For this Webster, long before his name was associated with dictionaries, had deserved well of his country. At an age when most men have barely begun their lifework, he had accomplished two things, either of which would have entitled him to a place in history.

First, Noah Webster, perhaps more than any other single citizen, had labored and agitated for the calling together of the Constitutional Convention itself. From the moment of the defeat of Cornwallis, this man, by turns schoolmaster, lecturer, pamphleteer, and publisher of schoolbooks from his own pen, had been possessed of the certainty that America had a future of her own, along her own lines distinct from those of any other country, and one which must grow out of unity in language, schools, and above all, government.

He was the author of a pamphlet, *Sketches of American Policy,* published in 1785. Chancellor James Kent, a distinguished contemporary and authority on constitutional history, maintained throughout his life that this pamphlet of Webster's was the first written proposal for a form of government approximating that actually framed by the Constitutional Convention.

SKETCHES

OF

American Policy.

Under the following Heads :

I. Theory of Government.

II. Governments on the Eastern Continent.

III. American States ; or the principles of the American Constitutions contrasted with those of European States.

IV. Plan of Policy for improving the Advantages and perpetuating the Union of the American States.

By NOAH WEBSTER, Jun'r. Esq.

HARTFORD :

PRINTED BY HUDSON AND GOODWIN.

M.DCC.LXXXV.

Courtesy, New York Public Library

Title page of *Sketches of American Policy*, with an initialed notation in the handwriting of Noah Webster, as follows: The following sketches were written in the month of February 1785, before any proposal had ever been made to remodel the government of the States. In May I carried one copy of them to Virginia & presented it to Gen. Washington. Mr. Maddison saw & read it at the General's soon after, & in November the same year, he, in conversation with me, expressed a warm approbation of the sentiments it contains. At the next session of the Legislature, which indeed began the same month, a proposition was made in the Assembly, for appointing the Commissioners, who afterward met at Annapolis & whose recommendations originated the convention at Philadᵉ in 1787. NW.

And during the next two years, Webster had spent a vast deal of his time traveling, lecturing, and distributing his pamphlet from New Hampshire to South Carolina — urging the adoption of a constitution which would bring such a government into being.

The importance of this contribution was freely acknowledged by Webster's contemporaries. Washington was merely the most prominent of the delegates who called at Webster's Philadelphia lodgings. Many others came to pay their respects to the opinionated young man. In after years both Jefferson and Hamilton thought him worthy of a controversial lance in the public discussion of fundamentals of the American political system. If Webster had never written a dictionary, he would now be given a place approaching that of Hamilton and comparable to that of, say, Robert Morris as a conspicuous figure in the founding of the Republic.

Webster was also remarkable for another accomplishment. He was the author—and the publisher and occasionally the only salesman—of a book which even then was more widely read and more influential than any other in America, the Bible alone excepted. Webster's *Blue-Back Speller* had already run through four editions. It was destined to continue in use for over a century, to sell over 70,000,000 copies, and to touch the lives of uncounted millions of Americans.

Webster's publication of the Speller, with his correlated activities in orthography, pronunciation, and usage, had already won its stiff young author the respect of America's leading citizens. The great Franklin himself had offered to turn over to this youthful Yankee pedant his uncompleted work on a reformation of English spelling, together with a font of specially cast type for a projected new pronouncing alphabet of the American language. Audiences in a score of cities up and down the coun-

PLATE I

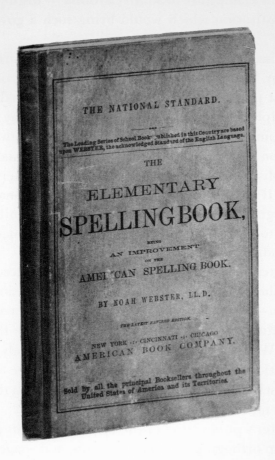

Webster's famous *Blue-Back Speller*.
Published in 1783, it has sold more
than 70,000,000 copies.

try had listened respectfully, if not always with enthusiasm, to the lectures of the gauche New England enthusiast.

But the Speller (its title was changed in 1788 to *The American Spelling Book* and later to *The Elementary Spelling Book*) was important to the ultimate fame of Noah Webster even more by reason of what grew out of it than for its immediate worth, great as that was. The Speller was at once Webster's first step in a career as lexicographer and the source of his bread and butter during all the years when he was, in one way or another, busy upon the great dictionary that bears his name. True, Noah Webster, perpetually in need of ready cash, was forever selling rights to the Speller for less than their full value, and since there was no federal copyright law, he was continually being bilked by pirate publishers who produced and sold great quantities of "Webster's Speller" without paying a cent to its author. But the book, with some assistance from two companion volumes in a series ambitiously titled *A Grammatical Institute of the English Language,* served to support its author during a long lifetime, and to gain a hearing for his peculiarly logical but, to many people, annoying ideas.

Noah Webster was a complex person. Basically a self-sufficient introvert with a tremendous store of energy and certain gifts for using that energy effectively, he gave an outward impression of pertinacious insufficiency which his acquaintances found extremely trying. All through life he was constantly, if unwittingly, alienating his best supporters, antagonizing political or sectional groups, rubbing audiences the wrong way. He was contentious rather than quarrelsome, self-confident rather than vain — but all too often people tended to see him in the less favorable lights. Though he never showed petty animosities on his own part, he had what amounted to a genius for arousing them against him. Fortunately for himself and the world, he was tough enough and self-assured enough to battle his way singlehanded against all opposition, and even on occasion to turn it to his advantage in attention-attracting controversy. But more important, he was the type that was spurred by dispraise to prodigies of labor and accomplishment.

His mind and character were shaped and tempered by two diverse groups of influences, each immensely strong: the New

Noah Webster's birthplace in West Hartford, Connecticut.
(Since the above sketch was made, by an unknown artist, the house has been completely restored.)

England Calvinism in which he was brought up, and the spirit of national independence which pervaded the entire time of his youth and manhood.

He was born Noah Webster, Junior, in West Hartford, Connecticut, on October 16, 1758. His father was a modestly competent farmer of that town, a justice of the peace, and on occasion an officer in whatever wars might come along. At home and in the primitive local schools, the atmosphere was compounded of hard work and a particularly austere, moralizing brand of Congregationalist piety. It was inevitable that the young Webster should acquire not only habits of industry, frugality, and rectitude but also the pompous disposition to sermonize upon those habits for the benefit of the world at large and the younger generation in particular. These traits, common to most Americans of his time, colored nearly all American published thought until well beyond the middle of the following century.

And running through all the boy's childhood and youth was another influence. Liberty was in the air and revolution was afoot. Along with the crudest of instruction in the Three R's, he drank in the notions of freedom and self-government. At Yale — where ordinarily a student would have got little but the driest of Latin, Greek, Philosophy, Mathematics, Rhetoric, and Theology — he lived in an air of excited discussion of theories of democracy and American nationalism. A new nation was born before his eyes; he had even a modest part in its birth. Later, he was able to help give it form and firmness. And all through his life the spirit of that nation was one of aggressive self-sufficiency with particular emphasis upon independence from Britain in matters not merely of government but of economy and thought.

Young Webster would have liked to be a lawyer (and later did have a fling at the bar) but lack of funds for law school sent him first into teaching. The difficulties and handicaps of that neglected occupation impelled him to write articles on the defects of country schools and schoolbooks. Then he compiled his Speller and himself secured its publication, not only to do something toward remedying the defects of which he had complained, but to supplement his own meager income.

## FABLE I.

### *Of the Boy that stole Apples.*

AN old Man found a rude Boy upon one of his trees stealing Apples, and desired him to come down; but the young Sauce-box told him plainly he would not. Won't you? said the old Man, then I will fetch you down; so he pulled up some tufts of Grass, and threw at him; but this only made the Youngster laugh, to think the old Man should pretend to beat him down from the tree with grass only.

Well, well, said the old Man, if neither words nor grass will do, I must try what virtue there is in Stones; so the old man pelted him heartily with stones; which soon made the young Chap hasten down from the tree and beg the old Man's pardon.

### MORAL.

*If good words and gentle means will not reclaim the wicked, they must be dealt with in a more severe manner.*

A page from an 1819 edition of *The American Spelling Book*, illustrating Webster's use of fables, with accompanying woodcuts.

But behind these immediate motives was a deeper purpose, and one which pervaded his entire life's work. Noah Webster believed fervently in his own mission to contribute to the future of the nation. His immediate field, as he saw it, was the building of a uniform and effective educational system, and his point of entry into that field the improving of the available books for teaching the use of the language. Hence the Speller, with its companion works and, later, other now-forgotten textbooks.

Perhaps even more important were the side roads of activity along which this work sent Webster at one time or another through all the years from 1783 to 1806. All of them led eventually to his great work as lexicographer.

These included wide travel to sell his books, lecturing and logrolling to promote them, countrywide lobbying for uniform state copyright laws to protect his property, writing pamphlets and articles, publishing magazines, practicing law, and a vast deal of study which led him farther and farther into the world of language, its origin, and its use.

At one period or another during his long life — even in the intervals of dictionary making — he found time to write extensively and well on languages and etymology, on history, politics, economics, foreign relations, international law, manners and morals, on epidemiology (to which he made a remarkable contribution) and, with something approaching Franklin's virtuosity, on phenomena in meteorology, horticulture, and the decomposition of house paints. . . . He could show turns of marked versatility in style: earthy, humorous vigor in an all-too-brief series of essays for rural readers published as the Hartford *Prompter*; flashes of rapierlike, sarcastic brilliance in controversy with his opponents; occasional moods of immense and winning dignity in response to criticism; clarity and eloquence in the revision of text for a Bible. . . . In his later years, when fame had offset the effects of his earlier partisanship and age had taken the sharp edge off his tactlessness, he was elected and re-elected to the legislature of Massachusetts and chosen first president of the board of trustees of Amherst College, of which he was one of the founders. And all these activities contributed to the making of Noah Webster's dictionaries.

# II

# THE MAKING OF
# A LEXICOGRAPHER

WE think of Dr. Johnson as an antique classic, the subject of innumerable anecdotes from the pen of the almost equally antique Boswell. But in Noah Webster's formative years Samuel Johnson was a living author. His Dictionary was the great authoritative work of its kind. His other books were current reading. His ponderous, reverberating style was the model for every young writer. The youthful Webster went out into the world repeating to himself the admonition from Johnson's *Rasselas*:

To fear no eye, to suspect no tongue, is the great prerogative of innocence, an exemption granted only to invariable virtue.

All his life he was fond of citing Johnson in his own support. In the preface to his great Dictionary he quoted Johnson's "The chief glory of a nation arises from its authors," and added, "With this opinion deeply impressed on my mind, I have the same ambition which actuated that great man" — i.e., to give celebrity to Franklin, Washington, Adams, Madison, Irving, and other American writers.

Yet all the while Webster was influenced by everything in the air that surrounded him to root out and extirpate the Johnsonian influence in this country. Americans of his day were obsessed with the idea of an independence from Britain complete not merely in a political sense, but in every sense. Extremists advocated the adoption of an utterly different language, Greek for preference, though the theologians favored Hebrew. And even such intelligent leaders as Franklin and Jefferson believed that within a few generations the American language would grow away from the English as Portuguese separated from Spanish, Swedish from Danish. Webster shared this view, and he was possessed of the compulsion to do something about it.

From Johnson and from the prevailing spirit of nationalism Webster took a vocation best expressed in the quotation from *The Rambler* which he later placed at the foot of the title page of his great Dictionary in 1828:

He that wishes to be counted among the benefactors of posterity, must add, by his own toil, to the acquisitions of his ancestors.

In the pursuit of this ideal, Webster found himself, almost before he was aware of it, involved in the study of language. Compiling a speller called for explorations into etymology and usage. Adding a reader and a grammar drew him into research in the history of our language, then of related languages, and so of language at large as a tool of human thought. He began to acquire a prodigious store of notes.

The farther he went, the more he was impressed with the inconsistencies of English spelling and their hindrance to the learner of the language. He agreed with Franklin and others that we needed a reform. Much of that reform could be accomplished, they felt, by restoring usage that had existed before recent and illogical departures from original custom. Spelling had been corrupted away from earlier and truly derived forms by the affectations of English writers. Even where the corruptions were of ancient origin and wide acceptance, they were illogical and needlessly at variance with good pronunciation. And now pronunciation itself was threatened with even greater damage at the hands of even more capricious meddlers. There had recently come into popularity, first in England and then in

NOAH WEBSTER, JUN. ESQ.

"Porcupine" portrait of Webster
from *The American Spelling Book*.

America, various pronouncing dictionaries, written by self-appointed, fashionable, but otherwise inadequate teachers of speech, including a man named Walker and the elder Sheridan. These popinjays were teaching would-be dandies that "egg yard" was the way Persons of Quality pronounced "a guard," and many other absurdities as well. Their influence was rapidly making it seem that the American mode of speech was barbarous and provincial, though actually the Yankee habit of saying "jine," "larn," and "heerd" was usage preserved unchanged from the Britain of our ancestors. Or so Webster and others contended.

Even Johnson's, though the best of existing dictionaries, was faulty in many respects. It had the inherent defects of its writer's individual genius; its definitions were in many cases inexact and its etymology obviously imperfect. Further, it was already far behind the times as the lexicon of a rapidly growing language. It had been largely limited to the listing of bookish words, avoiding almost entirely any truck with the words of commerce and trade. It was compiled when science in the modern sense was barely beginning to be recognized and at a time when all manufactures were still substantially of the handicraft order. During the latter half of the eighteenth century the arts and sciences had begun to grow — and their vocabularies with them — at a surprising rate. With them grew the standard of living of the ordinary man, particularly in America. By the first year of the nineteenth century the everyday citizen encountered in his daily reading hundreds of words for which existing dictionaries gave him no definitions — words in the advertisements of merchants, in the news reports of new discoveries, in magazine articles, pamphlets, and books. Any man opening his morning paper was likely to read about the trials of a *steamboat,* or to learn that *coral* was not (as his older dictionaries supposed) a

Courtesy, New York Public Library

Two facing pages from Noah Webster's copy of Johnson's *Dictionary of the English Language* (edition of 1799), showing Webster's annotations for new words, new uses of old words, new sources for etymology, points of disagreement (as at def. 1 of *toot*, v.; in his 1828 Dictionary given as def. 3 with the comment: "Not in use, and probably a mistaken interpretation").

plant growth but an animal product, to find what was the price of *ginned* cotton, or to discover what time the local *caucus* would be held. Further, Americans spoke and wrote a language which had changed, even in its usage of old words like *creek, bluff, demean.* There were hundreds of lusty new words and compounds, used every day in print, which had never appeared in any dictionary: *skunk, hickory, chowder, scow, handy, apple- sauce, bull-frog. . . .*

We needed, Webster saw, an American dictionary of the English language, adequate to the nation and the times. It should shape and mold our national language in a formative period, effecting certain reforms in spelling and usage as it did so. He had much of the material already in hand for such a work. The rest he knew how to assemble.

In later life, Webster credited the Rev. Elizur Goodrich of Durham, Connecticut, one of the trustees of Yale, with having suggested soon after the publication of the *Institutes* that Web- ster compile a dictionary. At that time, he said, he doubted his own qualifications for such a task, but as his work progressed he began to see his way more clearly, to arrange his materials more purposefully. And about 1800 he embarked definitely on his first lexicon, the *Compendious Dictionary* of 1806.

He had been — and all his life continued to be — an inde- fatigable accumulator of data. He had not merely the common New England trait characterized as "string saving" — the tendency to hoard anything that might come in useful — but his experience as a journalist had taught him to keep his notes thoroughly, carefully, and in the most exact order. His son-in- law and successor as editor of Webster's Dictionaries, Chauncey A. Goodrich (grandson of the Reverend Elizur), says of him in the "Memoirs of the Author" which form part of the prefatory matter to the *American Dictionary* of 1847:

All that he had ever written, all that had been written against him, every thing that he met with in newspapers or periodicals which seemed likely to be of use at any future period, was carefully laid aside in its appropriate place, and was ready at a moment's warning. He had also a particular mark by which he denoted, in every work he read, all the new words, or new senses of words, which came under his observation. He filled the margin of his books with notes and comments containing corrections of errors, a comparison of dates, or references to corresponding passages in other works, until his whole library became a kind of *Index Rerum,* to which he could refer at once for every thing he had read.

To deal with his enormous accumulation of notes, Webster had certain invaluable traits, some of them to a phenomenal degree.

An expressive blot, from Noah Webster's pen, annotates Johnson's definition of *Lexicographer.*

He was industrious, patient, yet enthusiastic. Dictionary making was not to him (as it was to Johnson) drudgery, but rather endlessly fascinating. He had a pedant's passion for perfection, but he was pragmatic about it: forever wishful to remake things aright, he was always ready to accept them, if need be, as they were.

He was receptive to a fault — especially to his own new ideas, but in no small degree to those of others. The defects of his

4 Any individual of a family descending in a collateral line; any descendant from a common parent or stock.

5. Branches of a bridle. Two pieces of bent iron which bear the bit, the cross chains & the curb. *Encyc.*

6 In gothic architecture, the branches of ogives are the arches of gothic vaults, traversing from one angle to another diagonally, & forming a cross between the other arches, which make the sides of the square, of which the arches are diagonals. *Harris*

7. A warrant or commission given to a pilot. *Laws of Massachusetts*

8 A chandelier. — ... — — — — *Ash*

Branch v.i. To shoot or spread in branches; as a plant, or as horns. To ramify;

2. To divide into separate parts, or subdivisions; as a mountain; a stream; or a moral subject; to ramify.

3 To speak diffusively; to make many distinctions or divisions in a discourse;

4 To have horns shooting out *Milton*

Branch. v.t. To divide as into branches; to make subordinate division. *Bacon*

2 To adorn with needle work, representing branches, flowers, or twigs. *Shenstone*

Branch'ed pp. Divided or spread into branches; separated into subordinate parts; adorned with branches; furnished with branches.

Branch'er n. One that shoots forth branches,

2 A young hawk when he begins to leave the nest, & take to the branches.

Branch'ery n. The ramifications or ramified vessels dispersed through the pulpy part of fruit. *Encyc. Ash.*

Branch'iness n. Fulness of branches. — — *Johnson*

Branch'ing ppr. Shooting in branches; dividing into several subordinate parts.

Branch'ing a. Loaded with branches coming out without order. *Mortimer.*

Facsimile of a page of copy for the 1828 Dictionary, in Noah Webster's handwriting, showing the remarkably small number of changes or revisions.

original dictionaries were those of a man all too ready to adopt new standards (as in spelling) which later failed of acceptance, or to believe in new theories (as of etymology) which were disproved by later and better-equipped research.

He was a natural linguist. Languages seem to have fascinated him from his youth; we find him, when he was barely out of Yale, offering to teach French to private classes. As long as he lived, he found it easy to acquire a mastery of foreign tongues; he collected them with a hobbyist's acquisitiveness.

In two respects he was outstanding among all lexicographers. He was, as Sir James Murray, the great Scottish lexicographer (of the *Oxford English Dictionary*), said of him, "a born definer of words." And he had the priceless faculty of being able to write a finished draft offhand and have it as correct as all the resources of his data and all his genius for detail could make it.

This last was a prodigious trait. Webster worked alone. With negligible assistance, he not only compiled but wrote out in his own hand the entire manuscript of a dictionary comprising 70,000 listings, a preface of textbook proportions and much supplementary material. The sheer labor of pen pushing in such a task would have been colossal, even if a man wrote at top speed, straight off, from clear copy already arranged in alphabetical order. The amount of time required for research on individual listings — to gather citations, to trace down etymologies, to establish usage, to determine the order of precedence among multiple meanings, to ascertain and to confirm definitions — is appalling to contemplate. And hardly less so is the labor that must have been involved in editing, alphabetizing, and other mechanical operations, clear down to reading proof, of which Webster himself carried the principal burden.

Yet back of this, Webster devoted some ten years of study and labor to the monumental and elaborately documented (if since largely disproved) theory of etymology which is summarized in his introduction. He spent a year abroad perfecting his research by comparison with English sources. He found time to engage in a vast deal of outside work and to earn a living by journalism and by pushing the sale of his Speller. It is fairly evident that there can have been little time left for long cogitation or knuckle gnawing over the business of writing his dictionary. Webster must—as the surviving pages of his manuscript show—have been a phenomenally rapid and assured writer. No other type of man could possibly have completed the great *American Dictionary of the English Language.*

He had in superb degree the talents and the temperament of the lexicographer. He already had at his command much of the material ready to go into such a work. The times cried aloud for a new and sufficient dictionary of the American language. It was very nearly the last hour at which that cry could be answered by any one man. Indeed, the very volume of the English vocabulary had already become so great with the growing complexity of life that probably the only man in all the world fitted to cope with it singlehanded was Noah Webster.

# III

# NOAH WEBSTER'S DICTIONARIES

NOAH Webster projected his dictionaries in a series or system, in what would now be called a news release to the New Haven papers of June 4, 1800:

Mr. Webster of this city . . . has in hand a Dictionary of the American Language. . . . The plan contemplated extends to a small Dictionary for schools, one for the counting-house, and a large one for men of science. The first is nearly ready for the press — the second and third will require the labor of some years.

Actually Webster's series proved to be in five parts rather than three. The first, or *Compendious,* dictionary did not appear till 1806. It was followed by abridgments for school use in 1807 and 1817. The large work — *An American Dictionary of the English Language* — was not completed till 1828. An abridgment of this for family use appeared in 1829, and the "counting house" dictionary followed last of all in 1841.

Of these, of course, the *American Dictionary* of 1828 was to prove the most important, not merely in itself but as the direct ancestor of that series of great revisions begun by Webster himself in his *Corrected and Enlarged* edition of 1841, carried on after his death by a succession of direct literary heirs of the great lexicographer and continued without a break of editorial succession through the famous unabridged editions to today's Merriam-Webster *New International, Second Edition.*

The 1806 *Compendious Dictionary of the English Language* was important and significant in its own right. It was no perfunctory abridgment of existing English works, as the few dictionaries hitherto published on this continent had been. Though it was a compact, duodecimo volume, making no pretense to rival Johnson's profusion, it flung down to Johnson's and to every other existing dictionary a challenge on five important counts: spelling (which Webster would reform), pronunciation (which he would guard against capricious change), etymology (in which he effectively showed up Johnson's shortcomings), modernity, and definitions. The first three of these are dealt with in an introduction by turns brilliant and abstruse, outlining those theories which Webster was later to develop more fully in the great dictionary of 1828. In the body of the *Compendious* he included thousands of words which were in daily use but not listed in any other lexicon. And his definitions, though brief often to the point of synonymy, proved brilliantly his special gifts for accuracy and precision in this, the most important feature of any dictionary.

It was already the custom to include supplementary tables after the vocabulary section of dictionaries. Webster, who had long since found supplements a valuable feature in attracting buyers to the Speller, went his rival lexicographers one better by including not only the obvious tables of moneys, weights and measures, divisions of time, lists of post offices and population figures, but also a brief chronological history of the world.

The *Compendious Dictionary* aroused a furor of comment but enjoyed at best a limited commercial success. Rabid patriots acclaimed it extravagantly, while the more eloquent intellectuals damned it with no less fervor.

Boston and Harvard — ultraconservative in spelling and ultramodish in pronunciation — would have none of the uncouth Yale prophet. They even objected to his listing colloquial words; there were too many words in the language already.

PLATE II

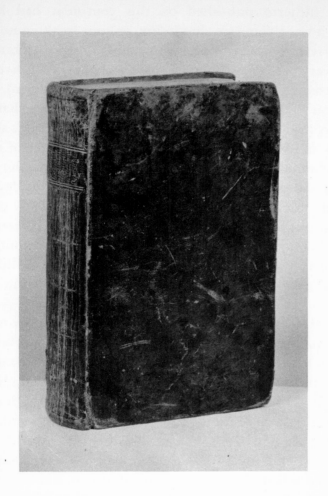

Noah Webster's first dictionary, *A Compendious Dictionary of the English Language,* published in 1806.

A

# Compendious Dictionary

OF THE

## *English Language.*

In which FIVE THOUSAND Words are added
to the number found in the BEST ENGLISH COMPENDS ;

The ORTHOGRAPHY is, in some instances, corrected ;

The PRONUNCIATION marked by an Accent or other suitable Direction ;

And the DEFINITIONS of many Words amended and improved.

TO WHICH ARE ADDED FOR THE BENEFIT OF THE

## MERCHANT, the STUDENT and the TRAVELLER,

I.——TABLES of the MONEYS of most of the commercial Nations in the world, with the value expressed in Sterling and Cents.

II.——TABLES of WEIGHTS and MEASURES, ancient and modern, with the proportion between the several weights used in the principal cities of Europe.

III.——The DIVISIONS of TIME among the Jews, Greeks and Romans, with a Table exhibiting the Roman manner of dating.

IV.——An official List of the POST-OFFICES in the UNITED STATES, with the States and Counties in which they are respectively situated, and the distance of each from the seat of Government.

V.——The NUMBER of INHABITANTS in the United States, with the amount of EXPORTS.

IV.——New and interesting CHRONOLOGICAL TABLES of remarkable Events and Discoveries.

### By NOAH WEBSTER, Esq.

From Sidney's Press.

FOR HUDSON & GOODWIN, BOOK-SELLERS, HARTFORD, AND INCREASE COOKE & CO.

BOOK-SELLERS, NEW-HAVEN.

1806.

Title page of Noah Webster's first dictionary.

Ordinary people were glad enough to applaud a truly American dictionary, but slow to rely upon it for guidance in the writing of their native tongue — which Webster would spell *tung*.

The school edition, too, sold only moderately well. It was not until 1817 that a new edition of this work, reset in larger format, could find a market. Yet the basic concept of a concise edition of a really authoritative dictionary, put out at a popular price for school use, was one of Webster's first, if least noted, contributions to lexicography. The student can afford neither the price nor the desk-space for an unabridged dictionary. Yet he, more perhaps than any other, has most constant need of an accurate definer and speller. He less than any other should be forced to accept misinformation from a casual compilation thrown together without benefit of current research and correction, out of extracts from some work so old that it has long since come into the public domain for any enterprising printer to copy.

All through the preparation of these earlier dictionaries, Webster was focusing more and more clearly the concept of his greater lexicon. The big dictionary was to be not merely "a large one for men of science," but a master work, surpassing Johnson's not only in range and modernity but in scholarly soundness as well.

Especially, Webster felt Johnson's all-too-casual etymology needed correcting; the Great Cham's errors were ten times more numerous than his friends supposed. Yet there was no master authority to cite in correction of Johnson's mistaken derivations. The earliest competent European works on linguistic science were yet to appear; philology as a science dates only from about 1818. So Webster was forced to construct a systematic theory of his own. Undeterred, in his innocence, by any appreciation of the true magnitude of the task, he embarked on such a creation, studying and comparing all languages of which

## No. XXIX.

HARTFORD, JANUARY, 1790.

### An ADDRESS to YUNG GENTLEMEN.

AT a time of life when the paffions are lively and ftrong, when the reezoning powers fcarcely begin to be exercifed, and the judgement iz not yet ripened by experience and obzervation, it iz of infinit confequence that yung perfons fhould avail themfelves of the advice of their frends. It iz tru that the maxims of old age are fometimes too rigorous to be relifhed by the yung ; but in general they are to be valued az the leffons of infallible experience, and ought to be the guides of youth. The opinions here offered to your confideration hav not the advantage of great age to giv them weight, nor do they claim the authority of long experience : But they are formed from *fome* experience, with much reeding and reflection ; and fo far az a zeel for your welfare and refpectability in future life merits your regard, fo far this addrefs haz a claim to your notis.

The firft thing recommended to your attention iz, the care of your helth and the prezervation of your bodily conftitution. In no particular iz the neglect of parents and guardians more obvious and fatal, than in fuffering the bodies of their children to grow without care. My remark applies in particular to thoze who defign their children to get a living without manual labor. Let yung perfons then attend to facts, which are always before their eyes.

Nature feldom fails to giv both fexes the materials of a good conftitution ; that iz, a body complete in all its parts. But it depends moftly on perfons themfelves to manage theze materials, fo az to giv them ftrength and folidity.

Bb2                                    The

A page from *A Collection of Essays and Fugitiv Writings on Moral, Historical, Political and Literary Subjects* (1790), by Noah Webster, demonstrating the author's use of reformed spelling.

dictionaries were available. Already proficient by 1800 in the classics and the leading modern European languages, he undertook Anglo-Saxon in 1804. By 1807 he had mastered twelve languages; by 1813, twenty. One of them was Sanskrit—until then an almost unknown tongue. Later he added six more, including the early dialects of English and German.

From these researches, Webster evolved a comprehensive theory of the origin, history, and relationships of all languages of western Asia and Europe. So impressed was he with the cogency of his own reasoning that after preparing the material for the first two letters of his great dictionary, he turned aside for ten years to compile a *Synopsis of the Affinities of Twenty Languages.* This work, completed in 1817, was never published, but its essence is contained in the introduction to the *American Dictionary* of 1828.

At the inception of work on that greater dictionary, Webster had sought the support of leading scholars and public men in the shape of advance subscriptions at $10 each. Response was disappointingly small. Webster had a meager income from royalties on his books, of which the only steady producer was the Speller. But even that — thanks to his earlier shortsightedness in disposing of rights — did not yield a comfortable living. Out of sheer economy, therefore, Webster moved in 1812 from urban New Haven to rural Amherst, Massachusetts. And there, during the years to 1822, he completed the greater part of the work on his big dictionary.

By 1824, with the end of his labors in sight, he realized the need for comparative studies in France and England to give the final touch to his work. On a thousand dollars, borrowed from a married daughter, he went first to Paris, then to Cambridge. Here, in his lodgings, in January, 1825, he finished writing the body of his dictionary.

"When I had come to the last word," he later wrote, "I was seized with a trembling, which made it somewhat difficult to hold my pen steady for writing. The cause seems to have been the thought that I might not then live to finish the work. . . . But I summoned strength to finish the last word, then walking about the room a few minutes, I recovered."

☞ Noah Webster. Esq. author of the spelling book, has given notice in the eastern newspapers, that he has completed a Dictionary of our language "at the expense of twenty years of labor, and thirty thousand dollars in money." He mentions that he made a visit to England, partly with a view to ascertain the real state of the language, and there discovered that no book whatever was considered and received in that country as a standard of orthoepy. He observes incidentally, that not less than 7 *millions* of copies of his Spelling Book have been sold. He thinks that the English dictionaries, are all, half a century behind the state of science, and hopes that his fellow citizens will be furnished with something better in the one which he is about to publish.

Contemporary newspaper clipping, from an unidentified source, announcing Webster's completion of his great dictionary.

The book was published, after some delays and disappointments, in 1828, under the title of *An American Dictionary of the English Language,* in two large quarto volumes: an edition of 2,500 at $20 a set.

From preface to last definition, it was a remarkable performance. The introductory section, embodying Webster's advanced theories on usage and derivations, was fated to have only a limited effect upon the language. But the body of the book, its vocabulary section, was an enduring work, instantly accepted as authoritative in its own time and destined to set the standards for all that is implied when people today begin any discussion with the words, "Webster says. . . ."

In the matter of orthography, Webster proposed reforms which have had only partial success. In his preface he demonstrated irrefutably enough that much existing English orthography was corrupt, artificial, at variance with etymology, and needlessly confusing. He would drop the useless letters in *imagin, farewel, crum, fether, wo,* and the like. He would write *ake, skreen, soop,* and *spunge. Wimmen* was "the old and true spelling" as well as that most accurately indicating pronunciation. These proposed changes look strange to the modern eye because they did not take, and Webster himself later dropped his advocacy of many of them. But on the other hand words like *music, center, color, plow, draft,* and *sentinel* looked equally strange to people of Webster's day, who were used to *musick, centre, colour, plough, draught,* and *centinel.* Considering the reluctance of the human race to change its ways, Webster's challenge to traditional spelling has had a great deal more success than a shrewd observer might have predicted for it in 1828. Seventy-five years later, not even Theodore Roosevelt as President of the United States had any comparable luck with an attempt — implemented with all the authority of executive directions to government departments — to introduce the simplified spellings with which Webster had failed.

With pronunciation Webster fared hardly better. His advocacy of the then-current American fashion had much basis in logic, and he pointed out with some brilliance and a good deal of biting scorn how capriciously English pronunciation had been (and was even then being) corrupted by self-appointed setters of a fashion in speech which would mark the difference

PLATE III

*An American Dictionary of the English Language.* Noah Webster's first large dictionary, published in 1828, in two quarto volumes.

AN

# AMERICAN DICTIONARY

OF THE

# ENGLISH LANGUAGE:

### INTENDED TO EXHIBIT,

I The origin, affinities and primary signification of English words, as far as they have been ascertained
II. The genuine orthography and pronunciation of words, according to general usage, or to just principles of analogy
III Accurate and discriminating definitions, with numerous authorities and illustrations

TO WHICH ARE PREFIXED,

## AN INTRODUCTORY DISSERTATION

ON THE

## ORIGIN, HISTORY AND CONNECTION OF THE

# LANGUAGES OF WESTERN ASIA AND OF EUROPE.

### AND A CONCISE GRAMMAR

OF THE

# ENGLISH LANGUAGE.

BY NOAH WEBSTER, LL. D.

IN TWO VOLUMES.

## VOL. I.

He that wishes to be counted among the benefactors of posterity, must add, by his own toil, to the acquisitions of his ancestors.—*Rambler*

NEW YORK:
PUBLISHED BY S. CONVERSE.
PRINTED BY HEZEKIAH HOWE—NEW HAVEN
1828.

Title page of Noah Webster's monumental dictionary.

between a gentleman and a man of the streets. The very commonness of a pronunciation, he contended, was the reason why it ought to be preferred. But time made a mockery of Webster's logic and eloquence; today for *deaf* we say *dĕf* rather than *dēf*, *ask* rather than *ax, further* rather than *furder,* as Webster would have had us do.

Equally destined for eventual rejection, but for a different reason, was Webster's fondly conceived and laboriously prepared theory of etymologies. The learned foreword, full of citations in Anglo-Saxon, Arabic, and Hebrew, proved in the light of later scholarship to have been built upon mistaken concepts and insufficient data. True, there were in Webster's time no other concepts, and his data comprised all that was obtainable in his day and on this side of the Atlantic. The scorn of later critics is akin to that which might be poured upon Fulton's steamboat because, forsooth, that inventor had not employed turbine engines and screw propulsion. Webster's rationale of language may have been primitive and ill-designed, but like Fulton's *Clermont* it got there much of the time; the great bulk of his individual etymologies were sound. And they were incomparably more so than those of Johnson's or any other dictionary up to Webster's day.

But Noah Webster's major, enduring contribution to posterity was not in the Preface at all. It was in the setting of a standard for what counts most in any dictionary — its range and completeness, its accuracy and timeliness.

In range, the *American Dictionary* far surpassed anything before its day. Its 70,000 listings included a whole vocabulary new to the pages of any dictionary — new words of science and industry; words of popular usage which the pedantic Johnson had scorned to admit to his pages. There were Americanisms, solidly welded into our tongue by a century or more of usage and already beginning to find currency in popular speech abroad. There were new forms with new meanings — *accompaniment, advisory, appreciate, editorial, insubordination* — and the only word Webster ever coined, *demoralize.* There were words whose exact meanings imperatively demanded establishment if a man were to do business, or his wife to trust the advertisements. These were not words merely of American usage; they were international. Now for the first time the merchant had an authority to define his requirements and expectations, whether he traded from New York or Madras or Rio or the Port of London itself.

And in the definition of this wealth of words, Webster proved his special genius—a combination of intuitive brilliancy with the infinite capacity for taking pains. Webster's immense mass of laboriously collected citations was the mine, his enthusiasm was the fire and his acuity was the craft with which he refined the pure metal of meanings, whether of words so long established that they had come to have a score of usages, or of terms right out of the latest findings of chemistry or astronomy.

In these two respects — by all odds the most important considerations in the making of any dictionary — Webster set a standard for himself and for his successors for centuries to come.

It had been the work of an ordinary lifetime. Webster was aging. He was 70 — a tall, slender man, addicted to the old mode in black knee breeches and silk stockings, "a curious, quaint, Connecticut-looking apparition." In the portrait by Samuel F. B. Morse, painted in New Haven just before Webster's European tour, one can see — as in all Webster's contemporary likenesses — those characteristics which made the man: the self-sufficient zeal, the combative pertinacity, the piety amounting at times to smugness, the passion for reform, the neatness and orderliness, the industry and thoroughness which had marked his lonely work down through the years.

Yet he had for his real friends a warmly human side. One of his first acts when the dictionary came off the press was to drive in his carriage from Hartford to Bedford, New York — 80 miles in cold, raw, late-November weather — to put advance copies into the hands of John Jay, the aged jurist, who had been among the few to respond to Webster's appeal for support twenty-one years before.

Jay and many other prominent men were quick to recognize and to hail the merit of Webster's great work. Letters poured in from every quarter praising it, often in extravagant terms. There were, to be sure, some dissenters and certain acid critics. Some of these were writers who had begun their attacks on Webster's first pretense to lexicography, as side lines to political opposition twenty years before, with satire and invective as their weapons. Now they resumed, seizing upon the obvious with shouts of derision for "Noah's Ark." Some critics were conservatives, alarmed at Webster's unorthodoxies of spelling, pronunciation, and usage. Many of these also had a personal distaste for Webster, whose persistent self-sufficiency was apt to impress even his admirers as ill-justified vanity. Boston and Harvard had by now acquired an added prejudice: "Another thing which has been noticed is his peddling his own production in person; had he addressed the public thro' the medium of the papers, or in handbills, with a specimen of his work, he would have been more successful." It was to be three quarters of a century before Beacon Hill and Cambridge could bring themselves to open the pages of Webster without a well-bred shudder.

Elsewhere, however, the *American Dictionary* was accepted with immediate acclaim. In Germany it quickly became, for its thoroughness, the standard dictionary of English. The British

PLATE IV

A modern interpretation, painted by Edwin B.
Childs in 1933. The artist based his conception
on a study of a multitude of descriptive notes,
of contemporary Webster portraits, and of the
features of Webster descendants.

PLATE V

*Noah Webster.*

Webster in old age. Engraved from a portrait painted by
James Herring in 1834.

overlooked its Yankee peculiarities because of its wealth of definitions — especially in the fields of science, manufacturing, trade and commerce — which were available in no other dictionary of the time. Even before an English edition was published (in 1830-1832) the British courts had begun to cite the Yankee work as an authority on points not covered by Johnson. And from then on, until the appearance of Ogilvie's *Imperial Dictionary* of 1850 (itself largely indebted to the American source) Webster was increasingly the arbiter of definitions throughout British life.

In this country recognition of the inherent excellence of the work itself was heightened by pride in American accomplishment. The press, with ribald exceptions already mentioned, gave the book fulsomely favorable notices. What was more important, publications and publishing houses bought the *American Dictionary* and started using it as an authority. Their example was followed by legislatures, courts, colleges, schools, and larger business houses. True, the price of the work ($20 for two quarto volumes) limited its initial sale to such establishments and to men of considerable substance. And even this distribution was materially curtailed by the fact that Converse, the publisher, went bankrupt as a result of speculations, so that the work — Webster's royalties included — was tied up in litigation; available copies were quickly exhausted; a new issue became impossible and much of the market had to remain unsupplied at the very time when national pride in an American dictionary was at its highest. Nevertheless, Webster's work quickly achieved an influence far beyond its limited circulation. It was *the* arbiter in places of authority, *the* reference work for writers, publishers, scholars, and other molders of public opinion.

This influence was shortly increased by the issue of an abridged edition (according to Webster's plan) in 1829. Com-

mercially, the abridgment had a happier fate than its parent
dictionary. It sold immediately and well, went shortly into a
second edition and continued to be a profitable reprinting
property until the middle of the century. Indeed, it was the only
one of Webster's dictionaries which sold largely during his lifetime. Culturally, it was important, too, for in octavo size and at
a popular price it was within the reach of ordinary people when
the larger work was out of print.

The 1829 abridgment had been prepared, under Webster's
supervision, by Joseph Emerson Worcester, an able scholar who
had already made an abridgment of Todd's Johnson. Worcester
had many of the gifts of a great lexicographer. But it is doubt-
ful if, without the foundation of Webster's work, he could have
attained, as he later did, the stature of Webster's most formidable competitor.

In 1839 Webster, though by this time past 80, began a revision of his *American Dictionary,* and with a vigor surprising at
his age pushed it rapidly to completion. This was published in
1841 (though the first printing was dated 1840) under the title
*An American Dictionary of the English Language, 2nd Edition,
Corrected and Enlarged,* but it soon became almost universally
known by the popular name of *Webster's Unabridged.* It not
only contained some 5,000 more words than the 1828 edition,
but its scientific terms had been carefully edited by Prof. William Tully of the New Haven Medical College, perhaps the
first of the specialist editors whose work has come to be essential
to the success of any modern dictionary.

Webster acted as his own publisher of this edition, mortgag-
ing his home to obtain funds. Despite his long experience with
publishing, however, he had never acquired any great degree of
astuteness in the production and marketing of printed books as
commodities. The work, in two octavo volumes, was priced at

$15 — a figure somewhat too high for ready sale. It did not move well. A considerable number of copies remained in sheets unbound when death overtook Noah Webster in 1843.

He died poor in worldly goods but rich in accomplishment. Lacking in almost every outward sign of greatness, he had yet succeeded—by combining curious, out-of-the-ordinary talents with enormous industry — in accomplishing, singlehanded, a whole series of great things the least of which would have entitled him to a place in American history. It has happened that the *Dictionary* has outlasted and outshone every other thing Webster did. This is due in part to the prodigious quality of Webster's own work during his lifetime. But it is also due in very large measure to sheer good fortune.

For the fate of the *American Dictionary of the English Language* after Webster's death might very well have been that of Johnson's great work: gradual obsolescence until the work became no more than a monument, a milestone in lexicography, and its existing copies mere collectors' items for bibliophiles. Noah Webster's "Ark," left stranded at his death, might have weathered untended into a bleached and useless hulk. Instead, a happy turn of chance caused Webster's great craft to be carefully preserved, rebuilt, and relaunched in his name by his direct literary heirs. Their direct successors rebuilt it again and again, each time improved and enlarged, so that today it sails the seas carrying a freight of words seven times as great as Webster ever knew.

PART TWO

New England Yankees

# IV

# ENTER THE MERRIAMS

IT is a favorite fallacy that the early New England Yankee was an ingenious, wily, and often unscrupulous trader — a ped-dler of wooden nutmegs at safe distances south and west of the Hudson — a seller of warming pans to the trusting natives of the West Indies.

Actually, the New England businessman of the early decades of this nation was more often a simple, frugal craftsman ventur-ing afield in sturdy confidence in his apprentice-learned trade and in his ability to manage, somehow, in spite of almost non-existent capital. Franklin was that way, and Revere, and the early shipmasters and cotton spinners and metalworkers and merchants. . . . For every one of them who gave less than full value there were dozens bilked by defaulting customers at a distance or by pirates of their work. Lacking the capital to be exacting in trade, they were forever eager to trust anyone who would buy their wares, to hand over money to anyone who would promise them a future delivery. And they made it pay, though often only after heartbreaking reverses and long years of self-denial. For, as the entire commercial history of New England proves, persistence, enterprise, and ingenuity are al-ways more profitable in the end than mere caginess in dealings with others.

To this too-little-appreciated regional trait, the world owes the rescue of Webster's work from the slow oblivion that threat-ened it upon his death, the successful popularization of the dic-tionary as a factor in national life, and the initiation of a systematic, continuing revision which has made the Webster Dictionaries of today an international institution.

In the early years of the last century there was in the village of West Brookfield, Massachusetts, a family of printers and bookbinders named Merriam. Two brothers, Ebenezer and Daniel, had started in 1797 with a secondhand press once owned by Franklin, a few cases of battered type, and a box of bookbinders' knives and rowels. They had done contract printing and binding, published a regional paper, and taken a hazardous venture or two at book publishing. On one occasion they bought, by trusting correspondence with an English printer, the type for a New Testament, only to find on its arrival that it was worse than useless and that their investment had almost completely vanished. On another, they innocently took the advice of mistaken counsel that anyone could print a *Blue-Back Speller,* and had unknowingly started to run off printings of Webster's work when they were called to account by Webster himself and readily said farewell to the major share of another investment. They were repeatedly fleeced by unscrupulous agents or held up by creditors who exacted exorbitant prices for mercy. They were forced to barter schoolbooks for calico, woolens, groceries, or produce. They apprenticed Daniel's four sons in Boston and Hartford and set them to work as soon as they were grown, sticking type, running presses, binding books. With a combination of frugality and daring, they printed books enough to keep themselves barely clear of debt: Perry's *Dictionary,* Watts's *Psalms,* another Testament, some pamphlets of sermons, Eaton's *Life,* a few primers, a Bible which cost them $4,000 when the market broke during the War of 1812. . . .

Daniel gave up and went back to farming, but his sons stayed in the printing business. George, the eldest, served a while with Uncle Ebenezer; then he and Charles opened a printing office and bookstore in Springfield in 1831. William and Homer started as bookbinders and publishers in Greenfield, outgrew that town's resources and moved to Troy, New York.

These sons were, understandably enough, a cannier lot than their elders in matters of trusting strangers, but they were no less daring as venturers in publishing. Both as separate pairs in the beginning, and as a firm later when three of them joined

GEORGE MERRIAM              CHARLES MERRIAM

*Cofounders of G. & C. Merriam*

forces in Springfield, they were able takers of chances in the printing of considerable editions of schoolbooks, Bibles, and lawbooks.

The brothers were all craftsman-trained in the production of books. They knew how to print and bind, and they had had to learn how to do so economically. In particular, they knew how to make full use of the then recently introduced stereotyping process, by which a publisher could print large editions at negligible cost for wear and tear on type equipment. This procedure favored the acquisition of books with an already-existing demand, so that large editions might be printed with good hope of success. Lastly, the nature of their business had forced them to learn the art of promotion both at retail (for they were book-sellers as well as printers) and at wholesale. They had a keen ap-

## G. & C. MERRIAM,

### SPRINGFIELD, MS.

#### CORNER MAIN AND STATE STS.

# BOOKS,

## STATIONERY

### AND

## Paper-hangings,

### Wholesale & Retail.

From a Merriam poster of 1842.

preciation of the value of printer's ink in selling, of artfully stimulated publicity, and of the influence of a judicious distri-bution of free copies.

By the late 1830's the firm of G. & C. Merriam was already well established in Springfield, with a prosperous bread-and-butter trade as booksellers and a growing business in the publication of schoolbooks, Bibles, and books of law, including especially the works of the then-rising legal luminary Joseph Chitty.

Toward the close of the 1830's the principal edition of Webster's Dictionary was the 1829 abridgment, of which the rights had passed by sale from Webster to his son-in-law Chauncey A. Goodrich, and so to the firm of D. & J. Ames, Connecticut Valley papermakers. The Ames firm, seeking to get out of the publishing business, offered their rights in the octavo abridgment to the Merriams, but at that time the brothers — though apparently tempted — did not have the capital to buy. It is probable, however, that the negotiations left them with a marked readiness to accept the later, and larger, opportunity which came their way in 1844.

When Noah Webster died in 1843, his heirs sold the unbound sheets of the 1841 edition of the *American Dictionary* to the firm of J. S. & C. Adams, of Amherst, Mass. But the Adams firm soon found that their purchase was more than they could carry. The dictionary, in two large volumes, priced at $15, was too expensive to move well. They offered all remaining sheets of the dictionary to G. & C. Merriam who, as successful booksellers, might presumably know how to dispose of the white elephant.

The Merriams closed, after arranging a simultaneous contract with the Webster heirs to insure their rights to publish revisions, and so became the owners of Webster's *American Dictionary of the English Language*.

It was a curious and — as it seemed — an inglorious resting place for the lifework of the great lexicographer. For all anyone knew, this was the beginning of the end of 60 years of scholarship — the first step in the disintegration of the greatest dictionary that had ever been produced. Its fate now rested with a pair of obscure, provincial publisher-booksellers — two men whose education, interrupted at twelve when they went out as apprentices, had never gone beyond that of the rural common schools. On all the record of its new proprietors, the great *American Dictionary* was due merely to become another reprintable property, for issue and reissue, unchanged amid ever-changing times, until there should no longer be anyone so undiscriminating as to want its musty definitions, its disregarded reforms, its disproved philology.

But the Merriams were, as it happened, exceptional men. At this time there were two of them — the George and Charles of "G. & C." Of the two younger brothers, William never joined the firm and Homer did not join it till 1855. For all the frugality of their upbringing, they had acquired (as printers do) a degree of education which, to judge from their written style in correspondence, would do credit to many a modern man of letters. They were already successful in a modest way, and they were obviously bound for still bigger things. What is more, they had three qualities which were to prove all important in the perpetuation of the Webster Dictionaries.

One was farsightedness. By the time they acquired the Webster rights, the two brothers had already decided to concentrate and specialize on some one or two fields. The dictionary was a desirable companion project to their increasingly successful publication of the legal works of Chitty. They were ready, too, to become more than mere reprinters — to embark on a creative career as true publishers.

Their second characteristic was a high sense of public responsibility. They were — and all their lives remained — practical philanthropists, with a propensity to take churches, schools, or other institutions under their wings and to finance them with contributions which often ran to $10,000 or more a year for one beneficiary. Somewhat the same attitude seems to have entered into their feeling for the Webster Dictionaries.

And the third Merriam quality which was destined to influence so largely the fate of Webster's work was the sheer ability to make money by the careful management of operations.

" When my father comes home in the eve-
ning from work,
Then I will get up on his knee,
And tell him how many nice lessons I learn,
And show him how good I can be."

**MERIT'S PRIZE.**

The bearer receives this as the reward of good behaviour and diligent attention to studies in school.

G. & C. Merriam, Print.....Springfield, Mass.

An award of merit, one of many designs printed by G. & C.
Merriam during the mid-nineteenth century and widely
distributed through schools, where they were awarded to
pupils for "good behaviour and diligent attention."

This was made evident — somewhat to the consternation of the Webster heirs — in the Merriam's first major move after acquiring rights to publish *An American Dictionary of the English Language.* The brothers proposed a revision and enlargement of the great lexicographer's work, in one volume, to sell at $6 a copy.

Sacrilege, cried the Webster heirs; $15 and two volumes were marks of respect due to the late author. But the Merriams knew what they were doing. They were merchandisers with a keen eye for a market and a sound knowledge of how to sell books in quantity. They saw that a lower price would so broaden the market that the total amount of profits, even at a reduced figure

The offices of G. & C. Merriam in Springfield in 1847.

per copy, would far exceed any previous returns on the Webster dictionaries. Events were to prove them right; within a quarter century they earned for the Webster heirs alone over $250,000.

But they had a very keen appreciation of the amount and quality of scholarship which would be required to preserve the value of their investment, not merely for the forthcoming edition but for generations to come. The new revision was to be prepared under the chief editorship of Prof. Chauncey A. Goodrich of Yale, Webster's literary executor and long-time confidant. With him would be associated William G. Webster, the author's son, Prof. William Tully, scientific editor of the 1841

CHAUNCEY A. GOODRICH
*Editor of the first Merriam-Webster, 1847*

edition, Prof. (later President) Noah Porter of Yale, S. W. Barnum of Yale, and a corps of specialists, including the Rev. James Murdock of Andover (Ecclesiastical History), Prof. Silliman of Yale (Chemistry), Prof. Stanley of Yale (Mathematics), James D. Dana, editor of the *American Journal of Sciences and Arts* (Geology), E. C. Herrick of Yale (Astronomy) and Nathaniel Jocelyn of New Haven (Fine Arts), and (for Law) the Hon. Elizur Goodrich of Yale, father of the editor and son of that clergyman who had first suggested the idea of a dictionary to Noah Webster, in the early years of the Republic.

Here, coming from a pair of plain, simple, matter-of-fact New England businessmen, was a plan which embodied two of the great essentials of modern lexicography: continuity in editorship and organization of experts. Webster's work was to be carried on in the spirit he would have approved, under the direction of a scholar trained by the great lexicographer himself. And it was the businessmen who recognized that dictionary making was not and never again could be a one-man job — that it was a task calling for the organized effort of the best minds available, applied to the best material which could be obtained.

Goodrich was singularly fitted for the job. His critical judgment and good taste, combined with his family standing, enabled him to remove from the new edition most of the Websterian crotchets which still remained from the original (1828) work. He was a trained lexicographer, an able organizer and co-ordinator of the work of others, and himself a man of profound knowledge.

The new work, *An American Dictionary of the English Language (New Revised Edition)* appeared in 1847 — first of a succession of Merriam-Webster Dictionaries that has now reached its hundredth year. The book contained some 85,000 entries in the main vocabulary section — 10,000 more than the edition of 1841 — together with new supplementary features.

Its success was immediate. President Polk, Zachary Taylor, Millard Fillmore, 31 senators and innumerable other prominent men hailed it with endorsements that read like a copy writer's dream. One hundred and four members of Congress signed a statement saying, "It is with pleasure that we greet this new and valuable contribution to American literature. We recommend it to all who desire to possess the most complete, accurate and reliable dictionary of the language." The press was enthusiastically co-operative, from the *New York Tribune* to the *Phrenological Journal,* which adjured its readers, "Get the best. . . . If you are too poor, save the amount from off your

PLATE VI

*An American Dictionary of the English Language,* revised and enlarged, the first Merriam-Webster Dictionary, published on September 24th, 1847.

PLATE VII

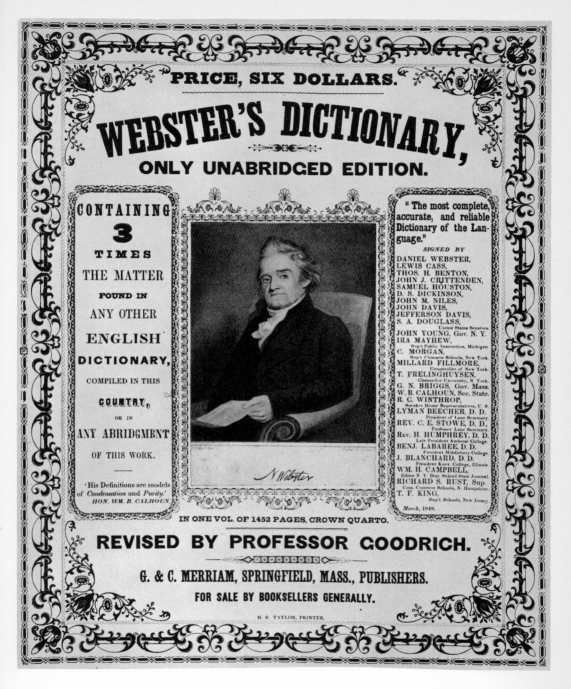

An early poster for the first Merriam-Webster Dictionary.

back, to put it into your head." Undoubtedly some of the gratifying recurrence in such reviews of the Merriam slogan, "Get the Best," was due to the ubiquity of Merriam agents, always ready to help a tongue-tied country reviewer with a striking phrase or two. But there was much other comment from distinguished journalists and men of letters which bore the unmistakable stamp of genuineness and spontaneity. An English scholar wrote lamenting half seriously "that the best dictionary of our language which has ever appeared should have been written by an American," and John Ogilvie said in the preface of his own British *Imperial Dictionary* of 1850 that Webster's was "acknowledged both in this country and in America to be not only superior to either of the two former [Johnson and Richardson, the outstanding British works] but to every other dictionary hitherto published."

Equally eloquent was the crackle of orders arriving on the desks of the Merriams each morning. Massachusetts promptly bought a large number of Webster Dictionaries for its public schools, and New York topped that quantity by a substantial margin. Courts, legislatures, and other government bodies ordered copies for official use. Newspapers, magazines, and printing houses installed Webster in their editorial and composing rooms. Business houses set the monumental Webster in their offices, and private citizens by the thousand wrote for copies or ordered them from their booksellers. America was thirsty for knowledge, avid for self-improvement, and the availability of Webster at a price within the reach of any ordinary man found instant response from the urban centers to the farthest settled limits of the country.

This success — and its continuance during the next two decades — was the more remarkable because it was achieved in the face of unusually vigorous and able competition. Joseph E.

Worcester published his *Universal and Critical Dictionary of the English Language* in 1846. It began the famous "War of the Dictionaries" which was to continue as long as Worcester (who brought out new editions in 1855 and 1860 and whose dictionary in later issues was sold for many years thereafter) continued a major factor in the field.

# V

# "THANK GOD FOR WORCESTER!"

NOAH Webster's spelling and pronunciation had been subject to attack since his first *Compendious Dictionary* of 1806. Sincere conservatives had joined forces with political rivals to poke acid fun at his proposed reforms. One of his more studious critics was the former associate, Joseph E. Worcester, compiler of the *Abridged* edition of 1829 and of the comparative table of varying pronunciations which appeared in the *Unabridged* of 1828.

Worcester was a scholar, temperamentally a preserver of the accepted, not a reformer of usage. As such, and by further virtue of residence in Eastern Massachusetts, he was *persona grata* to Boston and Harvard. In 1835 he had put together ("shoveled together," Webster's friends said) a condensed dictionary of his own, *Worcester's Pronouncing and Explanatory Dictionary.* Though much of it seemed to have been drawn from Webster, the younger man denied the older one's charge of plagiarism and in return twitted him on some of the more extreme spellings advocated in the 1828 *Unabridged: bridegoom, canail, ieland, naivty* and *nightmar,* among others. Partisans of Webster and Worcester took up the argument and bandied it about in the public press so lustily that by the time *Worcester's Universal and Critical Dictionary* appeared in 1846 there were all the makings of a first-class fracas, complete with rabid fans on either side, despite the fact that Webster himself was in his grave.

College students in their rooms at night debated the merits of

Webster and Worcester as hotly as their descendants now argue the relative puissance of regional football teams. The conductor of a local passenger train running into Worcester, from which city branch lines ran out to various towns including Webster, Mass., was in the jocund habit of shouting as the train slowed down, "Worcester, Worcester! All change for Webster."

At first the rivalry had been confined largely to the authors and their warmer supporters. Then, with the appearance of Worcester's larger dictionary, the respective publishers jumped into the fray with all their resources in advertising and personal promotion.

Each publisher scurried around to secure the written endorsements of prominent men. The Merriams printed their long lists of statesman endorsers, and Worcester's publishers countered with a nearly solid line-up of New England college presidents, from which the conspicuous absence of the president of Yale was (they felt) more than atoned for by the presence of no less than three presidents and past presidents of Harvard, all pulling for Worcester. Merriam publicity made much of the impartiality of Webster definitions — implying very plainly that Worcester showed bias against the South and the Democrats — and ending with the Merriam war cry "Get the Best." Worcester's publishers retaliated with *16 Reasons for Subscribing to Worcester*, all of them intimating that Webster was a fraud. Worcester's dictionary appeared in a British edition with a title page which claimed that it was "compiled from the materials of Noah Webster, LL. D.," an acknowledgment which the Merriams hailed with broadcast howls of delight because (as they pointed out in a pamphlet entitled *A Gross Literary Fraud Detected*) it had failed to appear in Worcester's American editions. Worcester partisans, unable to get far with the alibi that the British-edi-

"Sporting Intelligence: The Battle of the Dictionaries" from
a cartoon in *Vanity Fair*, March 10, 1860.

tion claim had been inserted by an unscrupulous English publisher, fell back on an allegation that the Merriams were high-
pressuring booksellers with tactics which they characterized as
"a black page in the history of mercantile notoriety." And so it
went, with claim and counterclaim, endorsement and counter-
endorsement, blast and counterblast, until the "War of the Dictionaries" became a byword in the press.

Whatever Worcester and his publishers thought of this battle, the Merriams seem to have enjoyed it. They got, on the
whole, the best of the war. More newspapers supported Webster than his rival. Such publications as were unbiased tended
to favor Webster; the typical review conceded Worcester a
slight edge in matters of spelling and pronunciation, but
awarded the palm to Webster in the far more important matter
of definitions. And saleswise, the Webster dictionary gained
out of all proportion to its rival. Even in Massachusetts,
Worcester's great stronghold, when the school districts were
given their choice between the two dictionaries, their vote
went to Webster, 3132 to 112. There is every reason for credit-
ing the legend that George or Charles Merriam — or it may
have been Homer (who by this time was a member of the firm)
— was in the habit of exclaiming, "Thank God for Worcester!"

But Worcester's "pugnacious dictionaries" did much more
for the Merriam-Webster than merely to provide sparring
partners for a lively and profitable match. They were major
stimuli in spurring the Merriams to the great revision of 1864,
by which the Merriam-Webster Dictionary became finally and
indisputably the best of its kind.

Toward the end of the '50's it was evident that Worcester
was coming out with another edition — his third. As a first
countermove, the Merriam organization prepared a new printing of the 1847 edition, to appear in 1859. It was to be enlarged

# PICTORIAL ILLUSTRATIONS

FOR

# WEBSTER'S UNABRIDGED DICTIONARY.

*The figures given refer to the page in the Dictionary, where the word and its appropriate definition may be found. Where the page is not indicated, the word may usually be found in its appropriate alphabetical place in the Appendix.*

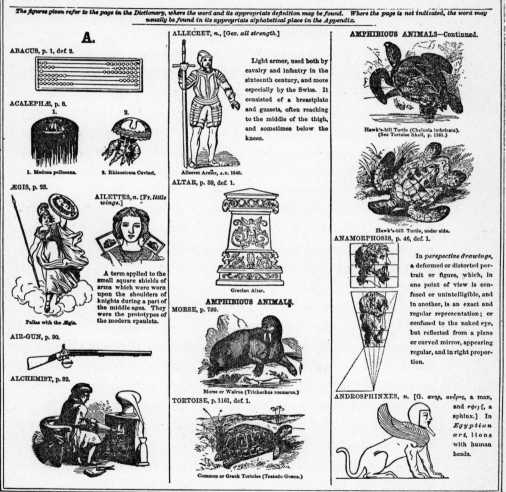

**A.**

**ABACUS**, p. 1, def. 2.

**ACALEPHÆ**, p. 8.
1.
2.

1. Medusa pellucens.  2. Rhizostoma Cuvieri.

**ÆGIS**, p. 23.

**AILETTES**, n. [Fr. *little wings*.]

A term applied to the small square shields of arms which were worn upon the shoulders of knights during a part of the middle ages. They were the prototypes of the modern epaulets.

Pallas with the Ægis.

**AIR-GUN**, p. 30.

**ALCHEMIST**, p. 32.

**ALLECRET**, n., [Ger. *all strength*.]

Light armor, used both by cavalry and infantry in the sixteenth century, and more especially by the Swiss. It consisted of a breastplate and gussets, often reaching to the middle of the thigh, and sometimes below the knees.

Allecret Armor, A.D. 1540.

**ALTAR**, p. 39, def. 1.

Grecian Altar.

**AMPHIBIOUS ANIMALS.**

**MORSE**, p. 730.

Morse or Walrus (Trichechus rosmarus.)

**TORTOISE**, p. 1161, def. 1.

Common or Greek Tortoise (Testudo Græca.)

**AMPHIBIOUS ANIMALS**—Continued.

Hawk's-bill Turtle (Chelonia imbricata). (See Tortoise Shell, p. 1161.)

Hawk's-bill Turtle, under side.

**ANAMORPHOSIS**, p. 46, def. 1.

In *perspective drawings*, a deformed or distorted portrait or figure, which, in one point of view is confused or unintelligible, and in another, is an exact and regular representation; or confused to the naked eye, but reflected from a plane or curved mirror, appearing regular, and in right proportion.

**ANDROSPHINXES**, n. [G. ανηρ, ανδρος, a man, and εφιγξ, a sphinx.] In *Egyptian art*, lions with human heads.

lxxxiii

Facsimile of a page (greatly reduced) of illustrations from the edition of 1859, the first American dictionary with illustrations.

by the addition of new words and new supplements. Dr. Good-rich threw in the cherished manuscript of a 300-page book of synonyms. Then it was learned that the impending Worcester dictionary would have illustrations. The new Webster, there-fore, must have illustrations — and more of them. Time would not allow resetting the entire book to make room for the pic-tures among the columns of text; it was barely sufficient for the procurement of 81 pages of illustrations, by prodigies of pur-chase and persuasion, to be inserted as a special section at the front of the book. The edition appeared with the title-page boast — literally true enough, if dubious in its sportsmanship — that this was the first American dictionary to have illustra-tions. A curious by-product of this expedient in make-up was that the illustrated appendix became so popular that public de-mand would not tolerate its omission when illustrations were run in with the text, as they were in all later editions. Indeed, it was only the pressure of space in the edition of 1934 which finally forced the dropping of this entertaining, if redundant, feature of the Merriam-Webster Dictionaries.

With the 1859 issue to hold Worcester at bay, the Merriams set themselves to prepare a completely new edition which should definitely and incontestably put Webster ahead of all competition. This undertaking called for courage. War was very evidently in the air. If it came there would be uncertainties of production, uncertainties of market, and who could tell what violent changes in the subject matter and treatment re-quired of any American dictionary? Nevertheless, the Merriams went ahead with their plans.

In the spring of 1859 the principal editors had been selected and approved by Goodrich. Of these, the chief was Prof. Noah Porter of Yale, Goodrich's right-hand man in the 1847 edition and his choice for successor to himself. It was a fortunate choice, for Goodrich died in the following year, and Porter was able to step into his shoes with the blessing of the Webster heirs, who were entitled by contract to approve the selection of any editor in chief. Dr. Porter had, moreover, the advantage of close acquaintance with the Merriams, whose pastor he had been some

NOAH PORTER
*Editor of the 1864 and 1890 revisions*

years previously at the South Church in Springfield. He was a man of very considerable learning, with which he combined an unusual talent for administration. He had, moreover, a breadth of vision which commanded the respect of all his associates; long before the edition of 1864 was planned, he had persuaded Goodrich and the Merriams that Webster's philology, brilliant enough in its day, was outmoded by more recent research and that it should be replaced by that of sounder scholars. On his advice they had selected Dr. C. A. F. Mahn, the distinguished German philologist, for this work and had commissioned him to overhaul the entire etymology of the Webster dictionaries. Mahn had partly completed this assignment as early as 1858.

The list of editors comprised a distinguished roster of some thirty university professors and scientists who were selected for outstanding competence in various fields, including chemistry, music, art, civil and military engineering, mathematics, law, medicine, theology, physics, metaphysics, archaeology, astronomy, geology, and applied sciences. To these were added a great number of editors, writers, and other literary men whose part-time co-operation had been sought and gladly given when the new work was projected. "The whole guild of literary men," said the *Springfield Union,* "was put under requisition . . . blank books, properly prepared, hung in hundreds of editorial sanctums, wherein any new term or contortion of a term might be jotted down. . . . Scholars and men of letters furnished long lists of words collected in the course of their reading. Besides these . . . there were from fifty to seventy-five persons, of whom thirty were regularly compensated" working at New Haven, Springfield, and Boston. These included full-time readers engaged to recomb English literature for citations, subeditors specially charged with comparisons, alphabetizing, and other highly technical aspects of dictionary making, artists and engravers (busy on the 3,000 illustrations) and special managing editorial assistants, including William A. Wheeler, a long-time Merriam wheel horse who acted as Boston contact with the printers.

The printing operation was a major undertaking. The book would be the largest single volume ever made in quantity. Even in its typesetting stage, it called for an unusual organization to keep up with the constant inflow of material from the corps of editors and to cope with the ceaseless additions, deletions, and changes that had to be made in already-set material as new words came in or corrections had to be made in old ones. (The Civil War, which had broken when the work was barely begun, brought many new words: *miscegenation,* for example, had to be crowded in by deleting a line of citation from *miscarry.*)

In this, however, the Merriams were fortunate. They had made a happy choice of printers in the firm of H. O. Houghton & Co. of Boston. The Houghtons proved so well equal to the difficult task of the new edition that despite the handicaps of wartime, hardly a day was lost in production through any delay in the print shop. It might be added at this point that the same firm, at The Riverside Press of Cambridge, has printed every edition of the *Unabridged* and of its successor, the *International,* since that time — and is still printing them.

The pattern of modern dictionary making was set in 1847 and 1864. And the man who set it, more than any other, was George, the eldest of the Merriams. He was a curious and an admirable example of the businessman among scholars. To the casual eye he was all business — a quietly industrious man who, long before the day of desk mottoes, put a sign over his roll-top desk, "Do It Now." He was unassuming, courteous to his clerical helpers no less than to his editor in chief. His correspondence reveals an endearing modesty: "Don't let my anxieties for progress trouble you. A business man's fidgets are not always wise." He had a fine, dry, humorous tact: "Put this in your triple condenser and boil it down to 13 pages." But he knew when and how to be firm: "We cannot & will not at this stage resort to delay." He had, moreover, excellent sense and judgment for deciding the fine points forever thrown up to him by scholars: whether to include this word and drop that; how to spell *savior* (*saviour?* — he finally bade them include both, in deference to ecclesiastical usage); which illustration to drop when a page had to make room for new words. And in matters of policy he showed wisdom and perception of the highest order. In October, 1863, at the height of the Civil War, when feeling throughout the North had mounted to fever heat, he considered the dictionary's listing of *slavery* as it had been in the 1828 and 1847 editions. The definition was accompanied by five citations, of which four were fiery quotations from abolitionist writers. He shook his head, drew a sheet of letter paper from the drawer of his desk and wrote instructions to the editors in New Haven to cut the citations to one which did not tend to arouse feeling. "We do not hesitate at all proper times and places to express our abhorrence of slavery, but this . . .is not the proper place."

Seemingly, too, it was George who was chiefly responsible for the Merriam's courageous decision to prepare a dictionary at all during this troubled period, to finance its publication (with a sublime confidence in public response) out of current funds, and to commit it to the press in early 1864 while the War was still on. He was the determined, purposeful one; Charles was a diplomat, a friend of all the world, an avoider of controversy — even (in later years) a little of an alarmist. Homer was scarcely more than the boy of the family. If Noah Webster was the great originator of the Webster dictionaries, George Merriam was their perpetuator.

PART THREE

The Endless Quest

# VI

# AN INTERNATIONAL
# INSTITUTION

*A*N *American Dictionary of the English Language, Royal
Quarto Edition, Unabridged,* appeared in late September,
1864. By October 1 the reviews were coming in. They were
for the most part careful and overwhelmingly favorable. Even
those publications which were still pro-Worcester usually acknowledged the outstanding qualities of the new Webster. And
indeed, from that time the Dictionary War began to wane.

It is interesting to trace, in the old Merriam correspondence
files, the ever-more-ready acceptance of Webster among national figures. Statesmen, as we have noted, were always strong
Webster partisans. They may or may not have been competent
judges of the fine points in lexicography, but they were forth-
right in support of what they held, rightly enough, to be a national institution. ("Supreme in philology," said Daniel Webster of the 1847 edition, though he was certainly no philologist,
and General Grant, though no lexicographer, had no hesitation
in declaring as President that Webster was "the best dictionary
of the English language ever published at any time in any country.") Literary men were more discriminating. From the first a
few of them, like Whittier, had been unreserved in their support, but most had particularized, as did Bancroft, Horace
Mann, and Washington Irving, that they preferred Webster in
the edition of 1847 for some one quality such as excellence in definitions, but had reservations on spelling, and some, like Oliver
Wendell Holmes, Sr., had gracefully hedged. With the appearance of the 1864 revision, however, even the hedgers began to

Oak Knoll, Danvers,
18th mo 2, 1878

G & C. Merriam
    Springfield. Mass

Gentlemen. Your new &
revised Edition of
Webster's Unabridged
Dictionary, beautifully
printed & illustrated,
is worthy, in its extent,
of its great literary excellence
the unmistakable clear-
ness. of its definitions, &
the thoroughness & accu-
racy of its etymology.
I have learned. to trust
implicitly its author-
ity. Yours truly
        John G. Whittier

"I have learned to trust implicitly its authority."—*John G. Whittier.*

acknowledge Webster's leadership. Emerson, who had been brought up on Johnson and who knew Worcester well, wrote "I have learned from good judges the superiority of Webster's Dictionary." Whittier had "learned to trust implicitly its authority." Even Dr. Holmes, still no man to let down his friend Worcester, acknowledged regular use of Webster, and his son, the rising jurist, conceded step by step that he consulted Webster as well as Worcester. Indeed, throughout the remainder of the century there was evident a growing acceptance of the continually improved Webster (while Worcester became increasingly obsolete) which was capped, at last, by the public coming to grace of Charles W. Eliot, President of Harvard, who wrote in 1900, "The former edition has been in use in my office for the last ten years. The revision now happily takes its place."

But far more important, though less spectacular, was the acceptance of Webster in publishing offices, courts, legislatures, schools, business houses, and other official and semiofficial centers of usage. The Government Printing Office itself hung up signs for its editors, compositors, and proofreaders, "FOLLOW WEBSTER." New York newspaper practice, shortly followed by that of the rest of the country, centered around Webster. Textbook publishers issued millions of copies of schoolbooks based on Webster. The *Atlantic Monthly* (under Howells) followed Webster in the very heart of Boston.

The West Point cadets were furnished with a copy of Webster for each room — and required to keep it in good condition. Schools in state after state and city after city (prodded by a well-organized "adoption campaign" from Springfield) standardized on Webster. Legislatures made Webster their authority by resolution, and courts followed this lead, right up to the Supreme Court of the United States. In every executive department of the Federal Government Webster was the authority.

Concord, Mass<sup>tts</sup>
August 21—

Gentlemen,
                On my return
home from the seashore
a few days ago, I
found the stately gift
you had sent me to my
great delight. In my
youth my father gave
me Johnson's Dictionary:
long after in Cambridge
I became acquainted
with Mr Worcester, and
bought his book. Mean-
time, I have learned
from good judges the
superiority of Webster's
Dictionary, and am very
greatful to you for
the gift.
                R. Waldo Emerson
Messrs G. and C. Merriam.

"I have learned from good judges the superiority
of Webster's Dictionary."—R. Waldo Emerson.

As early as the end of 1870, indeed, the *New York Tribune* could report with literal truth, "The *Unabridged* is generally regarded as the dictionary of highest authority in the language, and has a sale all over the civilized world. It is regularly issued in London, and in English, as well as American Courts of Justice, is considered as the leading authority on the meaning of words."

Webster was rapidly becoming an international authority. It was in use throughout the Orient; 500 copies had been ordered by the Emperor of Japan; minor monarchs in a score of distant countries made Webster the official English authority for their realms: the King of Siam, the Sayid of Aleppo. . . . A learned Chinese sought (and obtained) the rights to base a dictionary of colloquial terms on Webster. . . .

No small part of this international usage was due to the intelligent handling of Webster in England and throughout the British Empire by the firm of George Bell & Sons, who had been British distributors since the 1850's, who brought out several British editions during the latter part of the nineteenth century and who have continued down to the present time to sell Merriam-Webster Dictionaries in Europe and the British Colonies.

By the '70's, then, the Merriams found themselves not merely proprietors of a set of publishing rights, but creators and custodians of an organization for the perpetuation of a great institution in both American and international life. Having made "Webster" synonymous with "dictionary" and so in many senses with "authority," they now owned not merely a property but a responsibility.

To carry this responsibility they needed the help of younger men. Charles Merriam sold his interest in 1877 to Ivison, Blakeman, Taylor & Co., who had long been distributors of the

An Old Sun Rising with New Splendor.

3000 ILLUSTRATIONS.

☞ "The appearance of this New Edition will constitute an epoch in the lexicography of this country. We point to it with a feeling of National pride."—*Literary Gazette*.

G. & C. MERRIAM,
Publishers of Webster's Unabridged Dictionary.

GEORGE MERRIAM.        CHARLES MERRIAM.        HOMER MERRIAM.

Springfield, Mass. March 24, 1865

Messrs. D. H. Tripp & Co

Gentlemen,—Can we not sell to you direct, to our mutual benefit, our new edition of Webster? Our wholesale rates are, 25% from List prices. From that, if a case is ordered, we make 5% off for cash. Our new edition is received with much favor, and for much of the time since its issue we have been unable to get the books made fast enough to fill our orders. For a first lot we would put you 12 copies at the case price, for cash.— We send by mail a copy of pictorial pamphlet which we supply, to our customers for circulation. By circulating these in your packages or otherwise, we think you would promote the demand, and find ready sale for the work. We shall be glad to hear from you by order.

Resp'y Yours

G. & C. Merriam

A sales letter to the book trade, in the handwriting of Homer Merriam.

Merriam-Webster Dictionaries. They put into the firm a young man of their own — Orlando M. Baker — who on George Merriam's death in 1880 became the dominant and driving spirit of the Merriam Company and eventually its president.

Baker, a positive, energetic type, bearded like some ancient prophet and equally outspoken, had almost immediately to deal with a major problem. Early Webster copyrights had expired; some others, on abridgments, had been sold; those on the 1847 edition itself would end in 1889. It was dismayingly evident that in due course any printer with time and equipment on his hands might be able to offer the public a "Webster" — of sorts. Time was to prove this all too true; in the 1890's a so-called "Webster" was issued by a somewhat-less-than-candid publisher, whose book consisted of a photoengraved reproduction of the 1847 *Unabridged,* with illustrations in the supplement lifted by a similar process from the edition of 1859!! And an examination of the shelves of the Library of Congress will show a whole bevy of "Websters," published at one time or another with various qualifying trade names. Some of these were properly licensed abridgments. Others were simply reprints of long-since obsolete editions. And others still were irresponsible hodgepodges of old and new masquerading as "Webster" to a public which had come to regard that name as the assurance of thorough scholarship and up-to-date revision.

To Baker, foreseeing this situation, it seemed the more imperative that the Merriam Company maintain the process of revision and modernization of the Merriam-Webster Dictionaries without a break, so that the authentic dictionaries in their series might be recognized (at least by those who looked farther than the name "Webster") for their modernity and completeness.

Accordingly a program of revision was begun in the late 1870's. There was already in existence a small permanent staff.

Dr. Porter had been retained on salary since completion of the 1864 edition to give a continuing portion of his time as editor

A Merriam advertisement of the 1890's, warning the public of spurious and obsolete "Webster" Dictionaries.

in chief; Mahn, too, was kept busy on etymologies as new words came in and were filed for future editions. On his death, Mahn was succeeded by Prof. Edward S. Sheldon of Harvard.

The program contemplated a thoroughgoing revision, comparable to that of 1864, but since the preparation of this would be a matter of years, there were in the interim three new editions of the existing work, modernized by new material in added sections.

The first of these, issued in 1879, was notable for a New Words section of some 4,500 entries, as well as for a biographical supplement listing 10,000 noteworthy persons — a landmark in dictionary making. The book also embodied numerous minor changes in the material of the main section. Data for these additions and emendations had been accumulated partly by the labors of the editorial staff in research (the beginning of present-day practice) and partly as a result of correspondence.

From the first appearance of the 1864 revision users everywhere had started writing suggestions. Such letters varied from a clergyman's aggrieved demand for the inclusion of the theologians' technical term *cognize,* to Mark Twain's characteristic comment some years later on the etymology of *stateroom*:

While [in 1840] it is possibly true that there were passenger packets with no more than 30 staterooms, certainly they were not named for the states, but only *numbered.* And this was safe and right. With 15 state names on a side, it would have taken a man the rest of the night to find his own, even if sober, which he wasn't, in those days. Five men per night would have blundered into the wrong cabins and gotten themselves shot. To men in proper condition, names would enlarge, contract. The letters would fuse together, then melt apart and wriggle, and no [one could tell] Missouri and Mississippi apart. The swift multiplication of inquests would cause delay and provoke comment & injure business.

A new edition of the 1864 book, brought out in 1882, was one specially prepared for the subscription trade, with a History of the United States, in four divisions, by the well-known

Hartford, March 1, 1891

Messrs G. & C. Merriam & Co —
    Gentlemen:

    A Dictionary is the most awe-inspiring of all books, it knows so much; & this one is to me the most awe-inspiring of all Dictionaries, because it exhausts knowledge, apparently. It has gone around like a sun, & spied out everything & lit it up. This is a wonderful book — the most wonderful that I know of, ~~when~~ when I think over the impressive fact that if it had been builded by one man instead of a hundred he would have had to begin it a thousand years ago in order to have it ready for ~~publication~~ publication to-day.

    I thank you very sincerely for the majestic volume, & am, gentlemen,
        Truly yours
        S. L. Clemens

An enthusiastic letter from Samuel L. Clemens (Mark Twain).

scholar and historian Horace E. Scudder. Many would-be purchasers of the Webster Dictionary were people with small in-
comes who did not find it easy to pay cash in full for such a work.
To them an easy payment plan was a much-appreciated convenience, as the increasing sales of each succeeding subscription edition have shown.

During the same period the *National Pictorial* abridgment
was revised, re-edited in harmony with the latest *Unabridged*,
and published by G. & C. Merriam through various editions,
eventually (in 1898) becoming *Webster's Collegiate Dictionary*.

The third new issue of the 1864 edition was out in 1884, with
an enlarged supplement of new words and a gazetteer of the
world, containing the names with proper pronunciation of over
22,000 places.

From the same era dates the Merriam participation in a joint
project unusual in the publishing world. The American Book
Company of New York (the result of a joining of forces of Ivison, Blakeman, Taylor & Co. with others) contracted with Merriam for sales rights to a series of Webster school dictionaries.
The Merriams undertook to maintain the editorial content of
these junior works on a standard worthy of the name Webster,
the American Book Company to publish and sell the books. Today, more than six decades later, the arrangement is still happily
in force.

From the start, however, the main project had been a complete revision — the creation of a substantially new unabridged
dictionary on the foundations of the old. Work on this had begun in 1880. With Noah Porter's retirement from the presidency of Yale in 1886, it was pushed forward intensively. Dr.
Porter, though by this time approaching 80, was still a man of
extraordinary vigor and unimpaired ability. Around him was

formed a group of associated and special editors which included 14 leading authorities for educational, scientific, technical, and

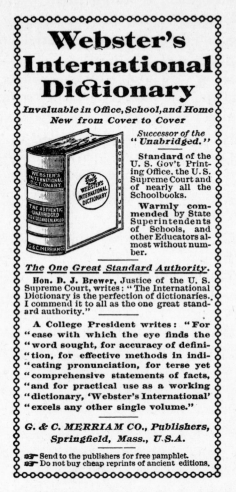

An early advertisement for the 1890 edition.

other special fields, 20 important contributing editors, and a greatly enlarged staff of editorial assistants at Springfield. Professor Sheldon, with the collaboration of Fick of Göttingen, further improved the book's distinguished etymology. All the vast detail of operation was under the supervision of Loomis J. Campbell, Walter Allen, F. Sturges Allen (later to be general editor of the Merriam-Webster dictionaries), and Asa G. Baker, son of Orlando, and destined later to be president of the company.

The undertaking was a formidable one in more respects than that of scholarship. The sheer magnitude of the project as a business operation was staggering. The 1890 revision entailed an outlay of over a third of a million dollars by the Merriams before a cent of return could be hoped for. No fly-by-night publishing concern could have undertaken it. Dictionary making had become a task that could be carried out only by a major business and editorial institution.

The new work appeared in 1890 under the appropriately distinguishing title of *Webster's International Dictionary*. It contained some 175,000 listings, an addition of 56,000 since the 1864 revision.

This increase was in part an index of the accelerated rate of growth in the complexity of modern life, but in part, too, a function of the broadened field in which Webster dictionaries were being used. They were standard equipment in business houses, consular offices, and educational and scientific institutions from Reykjavik to Punta Arenas, from the bourses of Brussels and Paris to the remotest copra-trading post in the Coral Sea.

From all the wealth of evidence of worldwide ubiquity of the Merriam-Webster, one story — often enough told — is worth repeating because it indicates how early Webster had come into use in out-of-the-way ports of the world, and how long even an old copy remained an everyday work of reference.

In April, 1898, just after the war with Spain had broken out, there came to the Merriam office a cable from Bridgetown, Barbados. It was signed "Stanley," a name which meant nothing particular in Springfield, and read:

> PAGE 1543 THIRD COLUMN COUNT DOWN 22 PAGE 1377 THIRD COLUMN COUNT FOUR BARBADOS PAGE 1501 THIRD COLUMN COUNT FOUR PAGE 911 COLUMN THREE COUNT 12 PAGE 637 COUNT 31 THIRD COLUMN PAGE 982 COUNT 17 FIRST COLUMN PAGE 761 FIRST COLUMN COUNT 15.

It was evident that this was a type of code message common enough in extempore cryptography. (See the Sherlock Holmes story *The Valley of Fear*.) Obviously it directed the recipients to locate words in Webster and fit them together to form a connected message. But comparison with the 1890 edition yielded only gibberish. 1884 and 1879 were no greater help. Finally, all the way back in the 1864 edition, the code fell into a clear pattern: TROOPER (Troopship) SPANISH BARBADOS THOUSAND MEN GONE NORTH INFORM. Merriam's forwarded the message promptly to Washington and later learned that the information of Spanish transport movements had indeed been correct and timely. After the war, Merriam's tried to locate and thank "Stanley." But Bridgetown and all its British inhabitants were disarmingly noncommittal; they had never heard of "Stanley" there. To this day the only clue remains the memory of a twinkle in the eye of a retired British naval officer in Bridgetown, who said that since Great Britain was a neutral he could not have sent the message, but that if he had sent it, he would not be such a fool as to admit it.

# VII

# "MAKE THE BEST"

WHEN George Merriam died in June of 1880, he left behind him more than a publishing property, more than an organization, more even than an institution of international standing. He left a principle and policy typical of his modest and thoroughgoing self. It was an ideal which — inveterate sloganeer that he was — he put into a three-word adaptation of the old "Get the Best" motto: "Make the Best."

The history of Merriam-Webster Dictionaries from the passing of George Merriam to the present is simply the story of a respected devotion to this ideal. New men appeared to serve it and were succeeded by others working toward the same end. New methods and new techniques developed as they were called forth by the ever-increasing magnitude of the task. Each new step was bigger than the corresponding one in the preceding cycle, required more manpower and more money, added more to the volume of the growing work and to its value.

The last of the Merriams retired from active participation when Homer, youngest of the brothers, relinquished the presidency in 1904 and retired at 91 to spend a spry old age in California. He was succeeded by Orlando M. Baker who, dying in 1914, was followed by H. Curtis Rowley, an able, competent administrator. Rowley gave way in turn to the dynamic Asa G. Baker who, having been "brought up on Webster" by his father, Orlando M. Baker, was an able lexicographer as well as a driving leader. And he was succeeded in 1934 by Robert C. Munroe, present president of the firm and moving spirit in today's smooth, efficient realization of the old Merriam ideal.

**HOMER MERRIAM**

*President, 1892-1904*

**ORLANDO M. BAKER**

*President, 1904-1914*

**H. CURTIS ROWLEY**

*President, 1914-1922*

**ASA GEORGE BAKER**

*President, 1922-1934*

In editorship, the Websterian succession has passed through a line of professionals who succeeded Noah Porter and who in many respects had more influence on the various revisions than their titular superiors, the editors in chief. Noah Porter trained the men who immediately succeeded him: Loomis J. Campbell, general editor of the 1890 revision — the man largely responsi-

**F. STURGES ALLEN**
*General Editor, 1898-1909*

**PAUL W. CARHART**
*Managing Editor, 1926-1933*

ble for its illustrious quality; Asa G. Baker, before he became president of the company; and F. Sturges Allen, an extraordinarily able lexicographer, the real genius of the supplement of 1900 and of the revision of 1909. Through these men, the Webster principles and influence were transmitted to Paul W. Carhart, pronunciation editor of the 1900 and 1909 issues, who was, in addition, managing editor of the *New International, Second Edition,* of 1934. From these, too, the Webster tradition of thoroughness in scholarship was transmitted to Thomas A. Knott, general editor of the 1934 revision; and to the present general editor, John P. Bethel. If the laying on of hands were an important rite in the making of lexicographers, it could truly be said that today's editors (and in all probability those of the measurable future) are the legitimate heirs in succession of the mantle of Webster. But what is more important, they are heritors by the laying on of minds. Webster personally influenced Goodrich and Goodrich himself chose Porter; they personally taught and inspired their successors, and so the influence of

WILLIAM T. HARRIS
*Editor in Chief, 1900 supplement
and 1909 revision*

mind upon mind has been passed on in unbroken succession through the chain of editors to the present day.

The first new issue after 1890 came in 1900 — an *International* with a supplement of 25,000 new entries, or 200,000 definitions in all.

Shortly after this was completed, work began on the revision of 1909, the *New International*. For this great undertaking a group of some 50 specialists was organized under the chief editorship of Dr. William T. Harris, United States Commissioner of Education, with ten revising editors headed by F. Sturges Allen and a corps of readers, proofreaders, and other assistants regularly engaged at Springfield. By careful typographic rearrangement and various other space-saving measures it was found possible to increase the content of the new edition to more than twice that of its predecessor, while still keeping it within the compass of one volume. The *New International* comprised some 400,000 entries; its added listings alone were nearly three times as many as all the listings in Webster's original *American Dictionary* of 1828. Though the dictionary aimed at rendering the best possible service to the average consulter rather than to the scholarly researcher alone, it was outstanding for scholarship as well — notably in Prof. George Lyman Kittredge's revision of James Hadley's *History of the English Language* which formed the greater part of the introduction and in Prof. John Livingston Lowes's masterly treatment of synonyms.

After the publication of the *New International,* a number of consultant specialists were held under retainer to help keep the institution's files abreast of the accelerated changes in the language and to assist in editing the *New International's* companion volumes: the *Reference History Edition* of the *New International* for subscription purchasers, the *Collegiate* abridgment, and the school dictionaries published and sold by the American Book Company.

The greater part of the consultants' work, however, was directed toward preparation of material for the next general revision of the *New International* itself.

This undertaking was begun in the middle '20's, eventually involved the activities of a staff — resident and nonresident — totaling upward of 300 members, and before the new work appeared in 1934 had called for an investment of some $1,300,000.

It was perhaps the most ambitious project in co-operative scholarship ever undertaken in America up to that time. It focused at Springfield the work of men and women located all over the world, wherever the best authorities could be found in universities, research organizations, laboratories, libraries, government offices, technical publications, or other centers of expert knowledge.

The editor in chief, chosen as early as 1926, was William Allan Neilson, then president of Smith College. A man of profound

**WILLIAM ALLAN NEILSON**
*Editor in Chief*
*Webster's New International Dictionary*
**Second Edition**

learning, Dr. Neilson was equally distinguished for his executive ability, his judgment, his knowledge of men, and his tact in leadership. With him was associated an editorial board consisting of Thomas A. Knott, general editor, Paul W. Carhart, managing editor, and Asa G. Baker, president of the company. Knott and Carhart were internationally known scholars; Baker, too, had been trained as an editor long before he came to the management of the company. The board set the pattern of the new edition, advised on the step-by-step assembly of the various groups of personnel who were successively brought into the work, acted during the intensive later stages of preparation as final arbiter of disputed points, and from start to finish decided matters of policy.

Once the over-all design of the new edition had been set, the permanent editorial staff was enlarged and set intensively to the assembly of detail. A corps of assistant editors was selected, with

THOMAS A. KNOTT
*General Editor, 1926-1935*

JOHN P. BETHEL
*General Editor, since 1935*

due regard for a wide assortment of general and specialized knowledge, but with one ruling requirement: each must have — developed and improved by experience — the talent which the great Murray had considered most important of all the qualities of Webster — that of a "definer of words." Among the members of this staff were Everett E. Thompson and Percy W. Long, veterans of the 1909 revision — the former still a mainstay of the Merriam-Webster staff; Lucius H. Holt, also an assistant editor of the 1909 book, and later (from 1935 until his retirement early in 1947) managing editor; Edward F. Oakes, currently associate editor, and John P. Bethel, today's general editor.

The words which were to constitute the bricks of the edifice, so to speak, were gathered by a corps of readers employed at an early stage of the operation. These included students from Smith and Mt. Holyoke — and readers of English-language publications as far away as Australia. It was their task to read source material, noting and marking new words or new usages of words, so that a card might be prepared for each such instance citing the use of the word in its context. The sources from which these citation slips were drawn included, of course, many of the more important books of fact and fiction which had not already been covered by previous research. Similarly, the principal periodicals were checked, including both general magazines and technical, trade, and scientific journals. Advertising pages, as well as pure reading matter, were covered. New terms and usages were drawn from reports published by official and semi-official organizations of every type. Glossaries of technical fields were fruitful sources of specialized meanings, as were slang dictionaries and other colloquial Americana. And, needless to say, the entire collection of citations was compared with the principal existing dictionaries and encyclopedias, both general and technical.

The citation slips were collected and alphabetized — that is, arranged in alphabetical sequence. Then the slips for those words requiring special treatment as new words or words with new meanings were segregated for the attention of editors.

Technical or other special-sense words were sent to the special consulting editors, of whom there were 207 in various fields of activity. They included such leading authorities as Joseph Sweetman Ames, President of Johns Hopkins; Fiske Kimball, Director of the Pennsylvania Museum of Art; the Rev. Patrick Joseph Healy of the Catholic University of America; Milo Smith Ketchum, Dean of the College of Engineering at the Uni-

PLATE VIII

The Editorial Department in 1933, at work on Webster's
New International Dictionary, *Second Edition.*

A portion of the Editorial Department today, in its quarters on the
second floor of the new Merriam building.

versity of Illinois; Roscoe Pound, Dean of the Harvard Law School; Albert Bushnell Hart of Harvard; and scores of others of equal rank.

On some subjects — particularly the scientific and technical ones — the task of special editors was a major operation in itself. For example, Norman Taylor, consultant on botany, and Austin M. Patterson on chemistry, handled (with the aid of several assistants each) tens of thousands of citation slips apiece. For each word they approved or revised an existing definition or formulated a new one.

Within the field of basic words of the English language, of course, the assistant editors at Springfield operated as expert technicians in defining. New words in colloquial usage were readily definable from a study of citation slips, which often numbered scores for each word. Similar study made perceptible new shades of meaning, new modes of employing old words. Frequently the editor's derived definition of such a word would be checked with an outside authority — a classicist or a columnist, a banker or a bibliophile, a publisher, educator, or a prestidigitator, according to the word and its principal field of usage.

Meanwhile, etymologies were separately prepared under the direction of Dr. Harold H. Bender of Princeton, and usage in pronunciation was checked with a corps of correspondents who included academic men, newspaper editors, writers, or others in close touch with daily life in some 50 carefully spotted cities of the country and in specialized fields of activity.

The text thus prepared was assembled and collated at Springfield. Duplications were eliminated and previous editions compared to guard against omissions. Multiple meanings of each word were arranged in proper sequence. Each entry was carefully prepared by one assistant editor and reviewed by another,

Shouts rang shrill from the boy's playfield and a whirring whistle.

Again: a goal. I am among them, among their battling bodies in a medley, the joust of life. You mean that knockkneed mother's darling who seems to be slightly crawsick? Jousts. Time shocked rebounds, shock by shock. Jousts, slush and uproar of battles, the frozen deathspew of the slain, a shout of spear spikes baited with men's bloodied guts.

—Now then, Mr Deasy said, rising.

He came to the table, pinning together his sheets. Stephen stood up.

—I have put the matter into a nutshell, Mr Deasy said. It's about the foot and mouth disease. Just look through it. There can be no two opinions on the matter. May I trespass on your valuable space. That doctrine of *laissez faire* which so often in our history. Our cattle trade. The way of all our old industries. Liverpool ring which jockeyed the Galway harbour scheme. European conflagration. Grain supplies through the narrow waters of the channel. The pluterperfect imperturbability of the department of agriculture. Pardoned a classical allusion. Cassandra. By a woman who was no better than she should be. To come to the point at issue.

—I don't mince words, do I? Mr Deasy asked as Stephen read on.

Foot and mouth disease. Known as Koch's preparation. Serum and virus. Percentage of salted horses. Rinderpest. Emperor's horses at Mürzsteg, lower Austria. Veterinary surgeons. Mr Henry Blackwood Price. Courteous offer a fair trial. Dictates of common sense. All important question. In every sense of the word take the bull by the horns. Thanking you for the hospitality of your columns.

—I want that to be printed and read, Mr Deasy said.

Reproduction of a page from *Ulysses,* by James Joyce, marked for citations.

on the general principle that no entry should go to press until it had been read by at least two people of the grade of assistant editor or higher. The entries were also checked for uniformity of punctuation, capitalization, and other points of style, and were subjected to a thorough proofreading.

Meanwhile, the illustrations — some 12,000 of them — had been overhauled under the direction of H. Downing Jacobs, art editor. Existing cuts were checked with an appropriate editor for up-to-dateness. Thousands of subjects were redrawn, often after lengthy search for authentic new data, and thousands of new terms were illustrated. Color plates were remade for the full-page inserts, and new ones were added. Proofs of all the illustrations were assembled with the units of text to which they belonged, for preparation of captions by Mr. Jacobs or other editors.

At all the steps along this route took place the infinite number of skirmishes which go to make up that lexicographers' war which the public never sees: the battle for space. No dictionary of any practical size can possibly include all the words ever encountered in print. No one-volume dictionary can give to every word the extended treatment (often verging on the encyclopedic) which its enthusiasts would like. The working editor must therefore be an expert craftsman in brevity — in putting the gist of each meaning into the fewest possible words consistent with accuracy, completeness, and clarity. Next, he must be a rigid self-disciplinarian to rule out, on his own initiative, words which, however intriguing to his imagination, have not earned a place in a dictionary, or which through long disuse have become what James Russell Lowell once called "the broken pots and dead kittens of speech." Lastly, he must be a good loser when, as so often happens, the general editor's decision in a borderline case of inclusion goes against some word on

A portion of the plate of *Representative Trees* (greatly reduced), one
of the more than 12,000 illustrations in Webster's New
International Dictionary, Second Edition.

which his heart is set. There are in the *New International, Second Edition,* some 552,000 vocabulary entries in the main part of the book, and it is scarcely an exaggeration to say that an equal number of potential entries must have been discarded in the process of making up the work.

The entries and illustrations, when all had been completed, were assembled in paste-up form, dispatched to the printers, set in type, and returned in galley form for proofreading.

i-n-f-l-e-c-t-e-d-n-e-s-s, n. ~~See -ness.~~

**6269**

i-n-f-l-e-c-t-i-o-n, i-n-f-l-e-x-i-o-n (-flĕk´shŭn), n. [L. inflexio, fr. inflectere. See inflect.] **1.** Act or result of inflecting; state of being inflected; a bending; bend; curve; curvature; angle; as, an inflection of the body, of a road, of motion.

**6270**

**2.** A change of mental or moral bent.

**6271**

**3.** Modulation of the voice; change in the pitch or tone.

**6272**

**4.** **Gram.** **a** The variation or change of form which words undergo to mark distinctions of case, gender, number, tense, person, mood, voice, etc. (as usually applied, ~~also~~ also, comparison). **b** A form, suffix, or element involved in such variation.

**6273**

A section of manuscript copy for Webster's New International Dictionary, Second Edition, composed of definition slips, numbered and pasted up for the compositor.

And so (paraphrasing Pepys) to press. That is, to the able hands of H. O. Houghton & Company's compositors and pressmen, to whose long-accustomed skill in producing the *New International* and its predecessors must go a great deal of the credit for producing a book of well over 3,000 pages swiftly, accurately, and with a minimum of close direction.

Mention should be made, too, of the S. D. Warren Company of Boston, suppliers of paper for the big books since the early 1870's. It is ever too easy for the publisher to think that it is he who has made a book. Actually a great deal of the reputation of "Webster" for legibility and usability rests upon the craftsmanship of the men who literally make the substance of the book itself.

PLATE IX

At the dinner in June, 1934, announcing the publication of Webster's New International Dictionary, *Second Edition*. Left to right: Asa G. Baker, President of the Company; William Allan Neilson, Editor in Chief; Thomas A. Knott, General Editor; Robert C. Munroe, Secretary of the Company (in December of that year made President).

# SEINING THE RIVER
# OF WORDS

*WEBSTER'S New International Dictionary, Second Edition*, was launched at a dinner to a distinguished company in Springfield on June 25, 1934. At that dinner a prominent speaker concluded his remarks, "If there is one satisfaction on this occasion, it is because we know that tomorrow morning you will begin another collection for another dictionary."

"Sir," said President Baker, "you are just a little too late. We have already started that adventure."

And in truth the lexicographer's work is a never-ending adventure, a ceaseless seining of the endless river of words. He does not create words; he catches and records them as they flow by in the current of active use. Our language springs from unnumbered sources — from techniques and sciences, from local dialects and metropolitan patters, from copy desks and broadcasting studios and the artless, unthinking innovations of millions in their everyday speech. New words and meanings bubble up out of life itself, trickle through the brooks of local or class or technical usage and come at length to the broad river of general print. Here the maker of dictionaries must cast his nets and tend them unceasingly, for the tide of the tongue flows without consideration for the convenience of man. The lexicographer — if he is to do an honest and thorough job of recording authentic usage and keeping his record up to date—can afford no letup, no breathing spell in his constant watch upon the flow of words.

It was evident in 1934 that the rate of growth in the language was increasing with the increasing complexity of life. Keeping up with it would require continuous application. Yet maintaining an organization adequate for this unending task was more easily said than done. To complete the 1934 revision the company had enlarged both its staff and its rented quarters far beyond the scale of its normal years of operation. It would be impracticable in ordinary years to maintain an enlarged staff or to

ROBERT C. MUNROE
*President of G. & C. Merriam Company, since 1934*

hold enlarged space. For in America dictionary making is not a state-supported or an endowed work; it must be run, like any other business operation, on its earnings. That was the problem which faced the company's new administration under President Robert C. Munroe, on the retirement of Asa G. Baker in 1934.

The solution they worked out was simple and logical: rounding out the Merriam-Webster publishing program by the addition of a limited number of closely related companion books, to be compiled by the large permanent staff while preparing material against the day of the next great revision of the *New International, Second Edition.*

PLATE X

Webster's New International Dictionary, *Second Edition*.

PLATE XI

Three Merriam best sellers: *Webster's Collegiate Dictionary, Fifth Edition; Webster's Biographical Dictionary; Webster's Dictionary of Synonyms.*

Already the company's operations included:

*Webster's New International Dictionary, Second Edition* — the mainstay of the Merriam-Webster business and reputation — sold through book-trade channels.

*Webster's New International Dictionary, Second Edition, With Reference History,* sold by subscription.

*Webster's Collegiate Dictionary*—the major abridgment. The Fifth Edition of the *Collegiate,* brought out in 1936 and embodying the essence of its parent work, the great 1934 revision, proved to be one of the all-time best sellers of the book trade.

Editorial preparation, for the American Book Company, of the two school abridgments: *Webster's Elementary Dictionary*, for children of elementary-school age, and *Webster's Students Dictionary,* for pupils of high-school age.

Now the company added two new principal books to its list:

*Webster's Dictionary of Synonyms,* brought out in 1942, was the product of years of labor largely carried on by the late Rose F. Egan, an assistant editor of the permanent staff and an able synonymist. Her brilliant introductory *Survey of the History of English Synonymy* is a landmark in that field, exceeded in importance only by the range, the thoroughness, and the acuity of treatment given to the book itself by Miss Egan and her assistants and advisers. Far surpassing all previous works not only in these respects but in modernity, the *Dictionary of Synonyms* has had a phenomenal acceptance both in this country and abroad.

*Webster's Biographical Dictionary,* which appeared in 1943, was similarly a labor of years in preparation by the permanent Merriam-Webster editorial staff with the assistance of 47 consultants advising in matters of pronunciation. The book lists some 40,000 noted men and women of all countries; its range is typified by the spread between its first subject in alphabetical order and its last: the book starts with Svend Aagesen, earliest Danish historian (fl. 1185): it closes with Vladimir Zworykin, contemporary Russian authority on television. Yet its biographical data are so concise and well ordered that, in some 1,700 pages, the book is readily usable as a desk reference volume — a utility achieved by no other work of comparable range and characteristics. And (what is particularly important in these days of far-audible communication throughout a world of increasingly common interests) it gives the user authentic pronunciations of names which range in origin from the American Indian and Aztec to Tibetan and Rhaeto-Romanic. Consequently the *Biographical Dictionary* has already had a notable success and appears likely to maintain its place as a working companion to the great Merriam-Webster *New International.*

Two other books should also be mentioned among additions to the Merriam-Webster list. One, published in 1944, is the *Pronouncing Dictionary of American English,* edited by Thomas A. Knott, general editor of the *New International, Second Edition,* and John S. Kenyon, dean of American phoneticians. It gives the student, whether American or foreign, authentic pronunciations of words, through utilization of the International Phonetic Alphabet. The other, *Picturesque Word Origins,* published in 1933, has proved a successful popularizer of interest in etymology.

These publications make possible the maintenance of a permanent editorial staff, continually employed in current routine work of cumulative value for the next great revision of the Merriam-Webster *New International.* That staff is larger than the entire group assembled for the complete rewriting of the *International* of 1890.

To house its operations, in 1939, the company, with Mr. Munroe at the helm as chairman of a building committee, launched a project for a new home for Merriam-Webster Dictionaries. This was completed the following year. It was carefully planned to meet the needs of both ordinary-year operations and of peak-year expansion.

The building, looking out over Springfield from the heights of Federal Street, has all the appearance of exactly what it is — an institution for the preservation and diffusion of learning. A fine, simple, gracious, Georgian brick structure, it stands like some university hall or library, surrounded by broad, clipped lawns and shaded by overarching elms. Its very street-number is significant; when the city officials approved plans for the building, they notified the Merriam Company that it might select any odd figure between 31 and 49. The Company chose "47" in allusion to the year 1847, date of publication of the first Merriam-Webster Dictionary.

Inside, the building carries out the promise of its exterior: it is at once scholarly and efficient, at once steeped in tradition and organized for production. The period furnishings and decoration of its lobby, executive offices, and board rooms are in the manner of an early nineteenth-century New England business house; its cabinets and safes contain a bibliophile's treasure of first printings, rare editions, and association copies of the great Webster works, and an autograph-collector's dream of letters that have come to the publishers from the great men of a century in American life and letters. Yet its operating space is laid out and equipped — from library stacks to cafeteria — with an obvious foresight of the concerted drive which will periodically be resumed whenever an augmented staff begins the rush of putting a great revision into print as the cumulative product of a century and a half — or, in time — two centuries and more of dictionary making.

The full force of this is borne in upon you as you visit the second floor. Here in one corner is the office of the present general editor, Dr. John P. Bethel, occupant (figuratively) of the chair once occupied by Noah Webster, Chauncey A. Goodrich, and Noah Porter, and the man more than any other single one to whom is due credit for today's smooth pattern of editorial operations. Beyond, in a large open room, are the desks of the assistant editors — scholarly desks, apt as not to be crowded with half a dozen open reference books at a time, yet orderly in the skilled dictionary maker's fashion.

But these take up only a portion of the available floor space, and the files and bookshelves, amply furnished as they are with a lexicographical library, are obviously prepared for a greater accumulation of material still.

Yet the "makings" of the next great revision have been kept well abreast of the developments since 1934 — breath-taking and world-shaking as those changes have been. On the shelves of the reference library you will find not only dictionaries, encyclopedias, glossaries, directories, atlases, and gazetteers, but reports and summaries, manuals and handbooks of everything from the treatment of displaced persons to the techniques of research in nuclear physics.

But the heart of the Merriam-Webster source material is its great citation file, daily added to by a corps of readers combing the press of the nation and the English-speaking world.

Consider this file carefully. To the outward eye it appears to be merely such another installation as you might find in the reference room of any library — section upon section of steel files, breast-high, each made up of 24 drawers for 3″ x 5″ slips,

*From a wood-engraving by Rudolph Ruzicka*

The present home of Merriam-Webster Dictionaries,
47 Federal Street, Springfield, Massachusetts.

and each drawer full of slips neatly typed and annotated or pasted up with clippings from books or periodicals.

Just a file? This long battery of metal drawers is, in a sense, one of the most remarkable "books" in the world. If an ordinary ring book of removable sheets is a book (which it certainly is), and if a business office's trays of loose-leaf records constitute a book (which, as any accountant will tell you, they do), then a filing cabinet of sheets arranged in order is a book. And a row of such cabinets, all containing one subject, is a book — and row upon row of them, one after the other, is also a book. In this sense, the Merriam-Webster citation file is a book, a phenomenal book — the greatest dictionary in the world today. It includes not only every definition from the 1934 edition of Webster, but every entry from years of organized reading of the world's representative source material, and thousands of citations from principal modern dictionaries, both general and technical. These extracts from other lexicons are all carefully labeled "For reference only." Webster makes its own definitions.

Great numbers of the citations are actually uses of new words. Sometimes there are whole bundles of citations for one new word such as *radar,* sometimes a small but significantly growing accumulation of uses of a word or a phrase out of the sports columns or *Variety,* or the advertising pages of the magazines. To each new word may be appended an editor's tentative definition with supporting authority if it is a technical term.

Then there are ever-accumulating new meanings of old words: *umbrella,* for instance, acquired a very special meaning in the last war as the protection afforded by a friendly air force to those beneath it, and one special, direful meaning of *atomic* has become the principal popular use of that ancient word. . . .

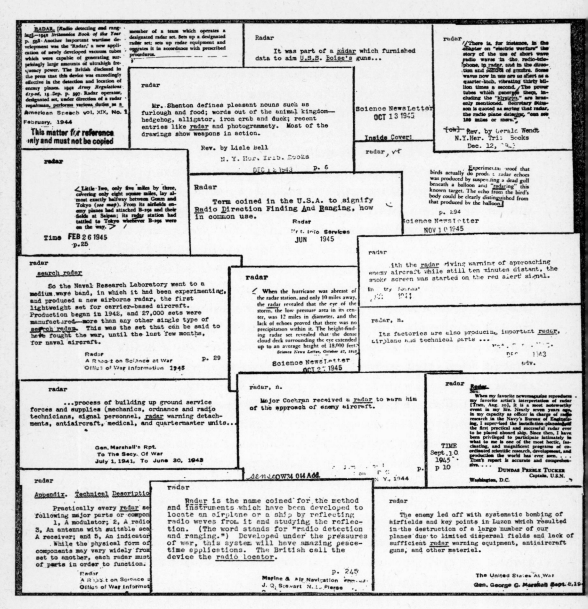

A sampling of the citation slips for *radar* showing the wide variety of sources from which they come.

This greatest of all lexicons, of course, will never see the light of print in its entirety. It contains hundreds of thousands of words which do not rate a place in any dictionary intended for the ordinary consultant. Aside from printability, the test of admission to the printed columns of Webster is twofold: usefulness and use.

A word may be undeniably useful, as many coined words are, yet if the evidence of citation slips does not show its use in more than one source or group of closely related sources, then it must stay on the waiting list till it takes wider hold — if it ever does.

Sometimes coined words gain an immediate vogue and by sheer accumulation of citations burst into Webster. *Jive* and *hep* are examples. Sometimes a word may lie unnoticed for years in obscure usage, then suddenly achieve such wide circulation that it becomes a household expression overnight: *boondoggle,* for instance, or *GI*. But many coined words, despite the fond hopes of their coiners, fail to show — in the Merriam-Webster citation file — that steady accumulation of slips which is the surest evidence of wide acceptance and continued use.

On the other hand, a word may have some usage but yet may not be useful to the ordinary buyer of a general dictionary. In this class come many technical terms. Chemistry alone includes tens of thousands of names of carbon compounds which have negligible fascination for the ordinary dictionary consulter, while many of medicine's jawbreakers are equally without reader appeal. An exception is *pneumonoultramicroscopicsilicovolcanokoniosis,* a listing that appears in the New Words section of the current edition of the *New International,* not because people at large have any interest in the obscure lung disease of which it is the name, but because they are forever demanding to see "the longest word in the dictionary."

It is essential to remember that the Merriam citation file is

BERNARD M. BARUCH
597 MADISON AVENUE
NEW YORK 22, N.Y.

December 11, 1936.

G. and C. Merriam Company,
10 Broadway,
Springfield, Massachusetts.

Gentlemen:

Answering your letter of December 5th,
the name Baruch is pronounced differently by
different members of the family.

I always pronounce it so that both
syllables are accented equally. The first syllable should be pronounced as if it were spelled
"Baah" and the second syllable as if spelled
"rook," pronounced to rhyme with "spook."

Yours very truly,

Bernard M Baruch

The Merriam method is to go to the source,
in matters of pronunciation.

not merely an accumulation of words, but rather a mine full of the ore of meanings, from which definitions may be refined. That is why it is thoroughly and systematically reworked whenever the Merriam-Webster is revised. Not only must new words be accurately defined. Every old word must be overhauled, too, and reconsidered in the light of its present-day usage. The user of Webster relies upon his dictionary not merely for accuracy, but for an accuracy that is complete and up to date.

Or a word may have dropped finally out of current use, so that the editors must decide whether on the record of citations it shall be kept in print (labeled *obsolete*) or can be safely discarded to make room for new material. Unfortunately for the lexicographer in his search for space, all too few words can be thus discarded. He may hungrily eye the space occupied by some obscure, obsolete term such as, say, *checklaton*: a kind of gilded leather jacket ornamentation that went out of style — and its name out of use — with the passing of the Elizabethan Age. It is a word completely useless to the life of today. Yet a glance at the citation file shows that *checklaton* was used by Spenser and others of that high and far-off time. So the editor cannot excise it without the risk of disappointing some reader of the old text, who may pause to consult his library Webster.

This responsibility to the user is no light matter. It has, indeed, grown heavier with every year of increasing acceptance of Webster. Courts, from the United States Supreme Court down, rely on the *New International's* definitions as a sort of common law: many a costly suit has hinged on a Webster definition, and many a citizen has gone behind prison bars or walked out onto the streets a free man, according to the light Webster's put upon his doings. The statute law itself is not infrequently phrased by legislators in terms straight out of Webster. Most daily newspapers and magazines, and nearly all the books that come off the press, are edited and printed in accordance with Websterian usage. Colleges and schools make the *New International* their standard, and, for nearly half a century, students have dug their way through pedantic obscurity with the aid of the *Collegiate*. In business offices the secretary corrects her boss out of Webster and the boss holds customers and contractors alike in line by citing how Webster says it shall be done. In thousands upon thousands of homes, youngsters lying sprawled under the table happily absorb from Webster information which teachers have striven in vain to teach them from textbooks. Clear through, indeed, to the everyday American's most trivial and jocose of doings, Webster is the unquestioned authority — the arbiter of his social-evening wrangles, the photofinish of his bets and wagers. In one recorded instance of a modern Webster error (an inaccurate typographic resetting of the formula for the date of Easter, which appeared briefly in one issue) an irate bettor claimed redress from Merriam because the supposedly infallible dictionary had let him down to the tune of five bucks, berries, plunks, smackers, or simoleons: a V, the half of a sawbuck. Yes, those terms too are in Webster — granules of the *New International's* burden of responsibility to be not only unceasingly right, but in tune with its time.

You might think so weighty a responsibility would lie oppressively upon the men and women who make the Merriam-Webster dictionaries—that the company's offices would wear a gloomy mien combining the more solemn features of a bank, a court of justice, and a surgical operating room. Nothing of the sort; the building on Federal Street has more the air of some pleasant university faculty club. There is good companionship, good talk spiced with banter across the lunch tables, good bridge enlivened by the comments of kibitzers before work is resumed for the afternoon. Thoroughness and accuracy are habits, not

PLATE XII

Reception Lobby; through the doorway, the "Merriam" room.

"Webster" room, showing Childs's portrait above Noah Webster's desk.

PLATE XIII

Robert C. Munroe at his desk in the President's Office, with
Ortrud A. Schulz, Assistant Secretary of the Company.

The Merriam employees at lunch in the Company Cafeteria.

burdens. Habits, indeed, in the antique sense of garments — worn as unconsciously as a craftsman's apron or a laboratory technician's smock. "You get so used to double-checking your facts," they tell you, "that you never think of working any other way." It is a heritage handed down from Noah Webster, and one which would win a frosty smile of approval from that exacting old precisian.

\*     \*     \*     \*     \*     \*

It is pleasant to imagine that sometimes, in the Lexicographers' Club in Heaven, Noah Webster, when he has been thundered down by Dr. Johnson in an argument about whose is the greater dictionary, may resort with an air of irrepressible satisfaction to his scrapbooks. One pictures him thumbing through endless clippings that begin, "Webster says," or "According to Webster," coming upon and reading aloud — ostensibly for Ogilvie, Murray, Worcester, and other bystanders but actually for Johnson's ear — this, which must be his favorite press notice:

There has never been a great nation with a universal language without dialects. The Yorkshireman cannot talk with a man from Cornwall. The peasant of the Ligurian Apennines drives his goats home at evening, over hills that look down on six provinces, none of whose dialects he can speak. Here, five thousand miles change not the sound of a word. Around every fireside, and from every tribune, in every field of labor and every factory of toil, is heard the same tongue. We owe it to Webster.

"Humph!" growls Dr. Johnson. "Pray tell me, sir, what is the date and source of that extract?"

"It is from *Glances at the Metropolis*," says Webster, patting the clipping back into place, "by the Rev. Charles Edwards Lester. He wrote it in 1854."

"But this," explodes Dr. Johnson, "is 1947! And nowadays," he continues, pointing to a pair of diffident, black-clad figures who have been hovering behind their beards on the outskirts of the crowd, "*you* owe it to the Merriams."

The over-all plan for this book was laid out by Robert N. Fuller, Executive Vice President of G. & C. Merriam Company, who worked closely with the author, particularly in the assembling and organization of the illustrative material.

The text of the book has been set in 12 point Baskerville. The illustrations have been reproduced by collotype and line. Of this cloth-bound edition there have been printed by The Anthoensen Press, Portland, Maine, 2,000 numbered copies on special rag paper, and a paper-bound edition on antique paper (not numbered).

# Date Due

| | | |
|---|---|---|
| ~~MY 31 68~~ | | |
| ~~DE 3 70~~ | | |
| ~~MY 13 71~~ | | |
| ~~MR 19 79~~ | | |
| ~~AP 2 78~~ MAR 2 0 00 | | |
| | | |
| | | |
| | | |

Demco 293-5